PRAISE FOR
CORPORATE HOMICIDE?

"*Corporate Homicide?* is a shocking eye-opener. Jerry Feingold does an ace detective job—as a latter-day Sherlock Holmes. With precise, riveting detail he investigates, presents the damning evidence—and nails it perfectly."

> — Ivor Davis, journalist and author of *The Beatles and Me on Tour*. Winner of the IPPY Gold Medal for Best Memoir.

"Kodak, Polaroid, Schwinn Bicycles—all dead and buried. I wondered what happened to them. At last, Jerry Feingold lays it all out with his authoritive and compelling research that reveals how these companies were destroyed by their own CEO's. A fascinating and easy read."

> — Ed Turner, Executive Vice President, Worldwide Operations for two Fortune 500 companies.

"*Corporate Homicide?* by author Jerry Feingold appealed to me personally and professionally. I enjoyed learning the history of many corporations that I remember in my younger years that seemed to always be there but are now sadly gone without explanation. Their rise and fall is vividly told and makes for a fascinating read about the rich history of corporate America.

"I found the many insights within these stories to be

a powerful tool to help me reflect on my own role as an agent of change. I recommend it as a great book about the human condition, with its truths and solutions applicable to the leader in us all."

— Nannette Percel, Teacher Consultant.

"In *Corporate Homicide?*, Jerry Feingold vividly describes how countless 'too big to fail' blue-chip companies self-destructed as a result of the hubris of bosses who deluded themselves into thinking they were untouchable. Like a clinical pathologist, Feingold peels away the subterfuge and takes the reader into the mind-set of these so called 'captains of industry' who were blinded by their own excessive pride and ego. Shockingly, Feingold reveals that while these highly intelligent corporate executives were witnessing their own train wreck, they were paralyzed when it came to avoiding those inevitable disasters."

— David Ostrove, Attorney, law professor, CPA inactive and financial consultant.

CORPORATE HOMICIDE?

The Remarkable Inside Stories
of How Some of the World's
Most Famous Companies
Destroyed Themselves

JERRY FEINGOLD

CORPORATE HOMICIDE?
by Jerry Feingold.

DEDICATION

This book is dedicated to those effective, wise, open-minded leaders who understand the words of Andy Grove, founder of Intel, who is famous for saying, "Only the paranoid survive." In my years in business, I am amazed how often I meet people in a leadership position who suffer from a "romance with the familiar" and are resistant to accepting advice.

I salute those of you with the courage to keep an open mind and be willing to embrace the wisdom of others.

I also dedicate this book to my wonderful wife, Ruthann, to our children Erik and Ellyn and their children Hannah, Stella, and Sloane.

ACKNOWLEDGEMENTS

I would like to thank my editor, Bill Thompson, for working with me on this book. His suggestions on the content and organization were important in making it better.

I also say thank you to Roland Dumas, one of my valued mentors, who helped me write this book.

A special word of recognition goes to Don Esters who has been a great boss, advisor, and valued friend for over twenty years and who set me on my exciting senior executive path.

TABLE OF CONTENTS

Thomas Edison: The War of the Currents 1

What This Book is About 5

The Kodak Corporation 7

Symptoms of a Potentially Doomed Leader 17

Five Ways Executives Go Off Track 21

    Mistake #1: Information Obfuscation 21

        The Ivory Tower and the Powerpoint Problem 21

        Nissan Motors 27

    *Mistake #2: The Yes Men Who Won't Tell the
Emperer He's Naked?* 37

    *Mistake #3: Power Corruption and Feeling
Invincible* 44

        Tower Records 48

    *Mistake#4: Loss Aversion The Pain of Loss Trumps
the Pleasure of Gain* 53

        Lego 56

        Polaroid 63

        Blockbuster 74

    Mistake #5: Later Rather Than Sooner 79

        *The "S" Curve and the All "The Time in the
World" Mindset* 79

        Schwinn Bicycles 84

        The Swiss Watch 89

Wang Laboratories 95

Xerox 100

Porsche 103

 The Kaizen Institute 104

 "The Machine That Changed the World" 113

 The Rescue of Porsche 117

Every King Needs a Jester 129

 Harman International 133

 Toyota 141

Executive Coaches 155

Conclusion 183

About the Author 189

Bibliography 191

Photo Credits 193

End Notes 199

OLD JOKE

The joke about three envelopes* is a classic business story about failed CEOs. It starts with the outgoing CEO who was recently fired for poor performance asking his new replacement to meet with him privately in his office. The departing CEO tells his replacement that he is going into a challenging job and hands him the key to the top drawer of his desk. He explains that if he gets into trouble there are three envelopes in that drawer numbered one, two and three that could help if he gets into a problem he doesn't think he could solve. The CEO puts the key in his pocket and forgets about it.

Things go well for his first six months on the job until the company starts to have problems and he worries about keeping his job. He suddenly remembers the three envelopes in his desk drawer. He opens the envelope number one and read a slip of paper with the words, "Blame your predecessor." Perfect! He makes up a story that pins all the blame on the last CEO, and he gets away with it.

Six months go by, and the company is in trouble. Once again, he opens envelope #2 that has a paper with the word "Reorganize" – yet another perfect strategy. He explains that all the problems will be solved once he gets rid of the non-performers in the organization and brings in new people with fresh ideas. It works, the company rebounds and once again he avoids taking the blame for problems he caused.

Naturally, six months later, the company is in trouble again. But, there is still another envelope. He opens envelope #3 to the last piece of advice: "Prepare three envelopes."

This joke originated in Russia where Khrushchev, having been forced out of power, hands three envelopes to Brezhnev, his successor.

PREFACE

Here's a list of some famous companies that are no longer on the Fortune 500 list:

TWA
Remington Typewriters
Woolworths
Pan-American Airlines
Napster
Sony Ericsson Phones
Borders Bookstores
US Steel
Studebaker
Zenith Electronics

A review of the Fortune 500 companies in 1955 to the Fortune 500 in 2014 reveals only 61 companies that appear on both lists. In other words, only 12.2% of the Fortune 500 companies in 1955 were still on the list 59 years later. The average life of a company on the

Standard & Poor's 500 Index of leading U.S. companies has dropped from 67 years in the 1920s to only 15 years today.

These companies didn't disappear overnight. Their downward slide into oblivion took a while. Don't you wonder what their CEO's were thinking during their slow-motion self-destruction? This book will explore how the behavior of CEO's led to the demise of their companies.

CEO's have a tough job. According to a study in the *Harvard Business Review*, two out of five new CEO's fail in their first eighteen months on the job. Many made fundamentally flawed choices. This book will explore some of these bad choices and suggest how the destruction of their companies was not inevitable, and, in fact, could have been avoided by more honest and realistic appraisals of their situations.

THOMAS EDISON

THE WAR OF THE CURRENTS

Thomas Edison is famous for the light bulb, motion pictures, and the phonograph, eventually accumulating 1093 patents in his lifetime. What is not common knowledge is his invention of the electric chair for executions.

After inventing the light bulb on October 21, 1879, Edison patented a system for distributing electricity in 1880. His intention was to benefit further from his invention of the electric lamp. He understood how anyone who had electricity in their home would have their lives changed. The Edison Illuminating Company, the first investor-owned electric utility, was founded in 1882 in New York City. This facility provided electricity to 59 customers in lower Manhattan. That same year, Edison started a similar power station at Holborn Viaduct in London that delivered electricity to street lamps and several private homes close to the station. Both the New York and the London generating stations provided 110 volts direct current (DC). Edison intended to provide DC power in cities across the United States with hydroelectric plants. He was certain this would guarantee a fortune in patent royalties.

The direct-current system generated and distributed electrical power at the same voltage used by the customers' lamps and motors. There were drawbacks. The system required the generating plants to be close to the customers and used costly, massive, heavy gage wire to compensate for transmission losses.

Edison recognized these limitations. It was very difficult to transmit DC over distances without a significant loss of energy. A rival company formed by George Westinghouse developed an efficient transformer that sent alternating-current (AC) power over long distances using much smaller wires. This was achieved by sending electricity out at a very high voltage that could then be reduced to the voltage needed by a customer. For example, today 120 volts are delivered to the home, but are "stepped down" to three different voltages used by various components in the home's desktop computer.

Alternating current generating stations were more economical because they could be larger to supply more homes, were less costly to operate, and the wires were less costly than the heavy gage wire required by DC transmission. Even though Edison knew Alternating Current was better than his Direct Current system, he persevered with his impossible campaign to discredit George Westinghouse. This created a bitter rivalry between the Westinghouse and Edison companies. Edison organized a vicious, highly exaggerated, scandalous publicity campaign focused on the "dangers" of high voltage transmission.

AC power distribution won the war because of the lower cost. But Edison would not go down without a fight. Edison was determined to ruin Westinghouse. He demonized Westinghouse's alternating current in a smear campaign that included ghastly publicity events where dogs, horses, and an elephant were killed using "deadly" alternating current. The campaign was so successful that New York State decided to use AC current as a capital crime deterrent and was first in the country to execute a human being with electricity. Edison called AC "executioner's current."

Edison recognized that AC was a superior system, but persisted nevertheless down the reckless, hopeless path of discrediting George Westinghouse's invention. His staff couldn't convince him otherwise. Edison's chief engineer, a brilliant Serbian named Nikola Tesla (the same Tesla the modern electric car was named after), told him that AC power solves the problems associated with DC of power loss, expensive wire, and the requirement of locating stations within a mile of the customer. But Edison didn't listen. He was certainly brilliant – maybe a genius. Was he incapable of recognizing he was wrong?

The execution of William Kemmler, August 6, 1890

WHAT THIS BOOK IS ABOUT

Next time you're riding in the passenger seat in a car, notice the driver's hands. She isn't holding the wheel rigidly; the wheel is being guided back and forth just a bit even on a straight roadway. Why is that? It's because the roadway is neither perfectly smooth nor perfectly straight. If these ongoing corrections to the car's direction weren't made, the car might cross over into oncoming traffic and crash. Or maybe the driver will realize a crash is imminent and violently overcorrect, thus crashing anyway.

That's the way it is in business. Senior management needs to constantly make corrections in the direction of the enterprise based on constant signals (what the competition is up to, what the customers think, changes in technology, financial indicators, employee morale), always assuring that the path being followed is in line with the company's strategy, vision, goals, and SURVIVAL. When this does not occur, the company crosses into oncoming traffic or overcorrects. In either case, the results of *ignoring signals and not controlling the company's direction* is failure.

The leaders of Kodak Corporation certainly received signals that digital photography was going to replace film. But they ignored those signals and continued down the path to bankruptcy. The publishers of *Encyclopedia Britannica* continued to stick to print when customers were flocking to CD-ROMs. The leaders of Remington, who made typewriters, saw the signs that word processing was going to eliminate their industry, but they ignored them and continued down the doomed path. Blockbuster didn't view Netflix's DVD's in the mail or movie streaming services as threats.

Why didn't they realize that their highly profitable businesses could not continue to flourish forever? Don't they know that trees don't grow till they hit the sky?

This book will explore organizations that failed principally because of senior management's incapability to admit they were heading off the track. A prime example is what happened at Kodak.

THE KODAK CORPORATION

The camera back then was a massive contraption that sat on a bulky, heavy tripod. The photographer needed a light-proof tent so he could apply photographic liquid onto thick glass plates prior to projecting the camera's image onto them. Then he had to quickly develop the "exposed" plates before the emulsion dried out. This process required him to use a pack horse to carry the tent, his camera, chemicals, tanks, water and a heavy plate holder.

George Eastman's camera changed all that when in 1883 he introduced his new product to the world; camera film in rolls. The Kodak company was created in 1888 when they advertised their first camera. It sold for $22. The average American wage then was about $3 per day. Each camera came loaded with enough film to take 100 pictures. The small, light Kodak camera could easily be carried and handheld during its operation. After all the shots were taken, the whole camera was returned to the Kodak company in Rochester, New York, which developed the film, made prints, loaded new film and then mailed the camera and prints to the customer. The Kodak ad in 1888 read, "You push the button, we do the rest."

In 1889, Eastman introduced roll film on a transparent base, which remained the standard for film. In 1892, he reorganized the business as the Eastman Kodak Company. Eight years later, he introduced the Brownie camera, which was intended for use by children and sold for one dollar. By 1927, Eastman Kodak had a virtual monopoly of the photographic industry in the United States.

The Original Brownie Introduced in Feb 1900. 245,000 were produced and sold for $1.00. It produced a 2 ¼ x 2 ¼ inch picture.

Eastman's company grew and prospered in Rochester, transforming a small city into a metropolis. Kodak's business headquarters occupied 200 buildings in a 1300-acre park.

By 1996, Kodak employed 145,000 people, and had revenue of $16 billion, profit of $2.5 billion. The Kodak brand was the fifth most valuable brand in the world, worth over $31 billion. But in 2012, Kodak declared bankruptcy. The staff was cut by 90 percent. The stock that sold for $57 in 1999, sold for $0.26 in January of 2012. Of the original 200 buildings, only 61 remain; the rest were either demolished or sold off. In 2016, Kodak employed 6,500.

Who would have believed in 1998 that three years later they would never take pictures on paper again?

There's a famous fairy tale that sheds light on what happened at Kodak.

The Emporer's New Clothes

In 1873, the Danish author Hans Christian Andersen published this fairy tale along with the Little Mermaid. The emperor has instructed two weavers to make him a fine suit of clothes. As they "dress" the emperor, the tailors convince him that his new clothes are fine and beautiful, though they will be invisible to anyone who is stupid or incompetent. The emperor believes them, and walks out among his subjects naked as a jaybird. But as he is the emperor, no one dares to tell him the truth.

On some level, the emperor must have known he was walking around naked. This brings up the subject of **cognitive dissonance**. It's the term conceived by psychologist Leon Festinger in 1954 to describe "the feeling of psychological discomfort produced by the combined presence of two thoughts that do not follow from one another". In other words, it's an uncomfortable feeling that comes from holding two opposing thoughts in the mind at the same time. We don't like to believe we may be wrong, so we ignore other people's input about things that are different than our pre-existing beliefs. Or simply stated, cognitive dissonance is a way of rationalizing mistakes or mistaken beliefs. Some people, when confronted by those who are trying to persuade them to change their opinions or plans, will dig in their heels and refuse to change their position. An everyday example would be the obese person who knows that going on a diet and exercising would make him look better and feel better. But he convinces himself that being overweight isn't really that bad. He justifies his behavior by denying the truth.

Kodak at its peak dominated the photographic world. The Kodak name back then was a household name, just as Apple and Microsoft are today. Aside from the cameras they sold worldwide to produce "Kodak Moments," they also were heavily involved in the motion picture industry by setting the 35 mm film standard, and introduced the 16 mm film format for home movies. Kodak worked with the military in development of cameras for reconnaissance planes and spy satellites. Kodak also entered the markets of document scanners, data storage systems (optical, tape, and disk), printers, inkjet printing presses, microfilm/microfiche equipment, photograph kiosks, medical radiographic diagnostic imaging devices and photocopiers.

One of Kodak's most impressive inventions was the digital camera they introduced in 1975. Kodak scientists invented this revolution to photography and patented it. But instead of aggressively marketing their new digital cameras, they shelved the idea, fearing it would hurt their chemical and film businesses. In 1988 Kodak acquired Sterling Drug, the American global pharmaceutical company, for $5.1 billion. Kodak was fully aware at that time of all the digital products entering the markets.

In preparation for writing this book, I spoke with Dr. K. Bradley Paxton, PhD, former VP & GM of the Electronic Photography Division and Director of the Kodak Electronic Imaging Research Laboratories. His groups helped develop many digital imaging products, including the digital camera. In 1989, he described the digital camera to Kodak's CEO and other top management. He described a camera that could take almost unlimited shots, delete the unwanted ones, and permanently store the rest. The reaction was they didn't like the idea having a camera that didn't use film or intentionally "losing print sales."

The CEO at that time knew that Kodak's profits came from what was essentially a chemical company—a company that supported the need to have film capture and print images. It was difficult to imagine a world in which pictures would no longer be kept in albums, but instead shared in social media.

Dr. Paxton was telling the emperor he was naked. The CEO believed that Kodak should continue its role as a chemical company and continue the infinitely renewable stream of $2.5 billion a year in profits. But at some level, he also knew that the digital revolution was inevitable. Like other sufferers of cognitive dissonance, he justified his behavior by denying the truth. Like the driver about to drift into oncoming traffic, he held the steering wheel stubbornly rigid and drove into a catastrophe.

Why would the CEO behave that way? Research has shown that the more effort and time invested in a decision or the forming of a belief, the larger the potential dissonance created if opposing evidence is discovered. A number of influences that, over time, probably reinforced his belief that Kodak should not change direction: He was in constant contact with executives from the chemical divisions telling him how good their divisions were doing. He may have been given distorted facts about digital photography being a soon-to-fade fad or a technology that would take decades to perfect. He may have been attracted and deeply committed to activities that confirmed his false assumptions. He may have been surrounded by yes-men.

One of the first published cases of cognitive dissonance was reported in psychologist Festinger's book, where he and his associates joined a group of UFO religionists in Chicago called the Seekers. Their leader claimed to have received a message from the leader of a planet named Clarion forecasting a great flood on December 21, 1954 that would end the world before dawn. The members of the Seekers took this revelation from Clarion seriously and prepared to leave Planet Earth on a flying saucer being sent to rescue the true believers. They quit their jobs and school, gave away their money and possessions, and some left their spouses. When the world did not end on that day, Festinger investigated how the disappointed Seekers reacted to the failed prediction. He learned they were not embarrassed or humiliated. He learned they didn't admit they were wrong.

The cultists believed they had saved the planet from the flood and wanted publicity to explain how their obedience and faith persuaded the space aliens to spare Earth for their sake. They had a new role and that was to make the whole world listen. Festinger concluded the Seeker's incredible response was not a need to admit the truth and change their minds, but to make themselves even more comfortable with their mistaken beliefs.

When it comes to belief systems, especially those that we have publicly committed to, we will rearrange our interpretation of data to fit the beliefs rather than change the beliefs. It's a bit like the blackjack card game where the term "Doubling Down" is common. In the business world, doubling down typically means to *engage in chancy behavior, particularly when one is already in a perilous situation.*

In 2010, HP Senior VP Brian Humphries said the company was doubling down on its investment in the Palm (remember PDA's?) web software operating system (WebOS). It failed.

In 2012 Apple's CEO, Tim Cook, said Apple was doubling down on maintaining the secrecy of new products. All the secrets of the Apple iPhone 5 were subsequently leaked to the media.

All these examples are forms of cognitive dissonance. A number of qualities can lead executives to behave that way.

SYMPTOMS OF A POTENTIALLY DOOMED LEADER

An overestimation of ability to make decisions

Psychologists Robert Hogan, Robert Raskin, and Dan Franzini, in their 1992 essay "The Dark Side of Charisma," describe the *Narcissist Manager* whose "energy and self-confidence and charm led him inexorably up the corporate ladder. Narcissists are terrible managers. They resist accepting suggestions, thinking it will make them appear weak, and they don't believe that others have anything useful to tell them. They are biased to take more credit for success than is legitimate. They are biased to avoid acknowledging responsibility for their failures and shortcomings for the same reasons that they claim more success than is their due.

"Moreover: Narcissists typically make judgments with greater confidence than other people...and because their judgments are rendered with such conviction, other people tend to believe them and the narcissists become disproportionately more influential in groups situations. Finally, because of their confidence and strong need for recognition, narcissists tend to 'self-nominate'; consequently, when a leadership gap appears in a group or organizations, the narcissists rush to fill it."

Reluctance to "give up power"

This is often associated with an inability to delegate and a tendency to micromanage—a need to approve minor expenses and a propensity to second-guess the decisions of subordinates.

A prejudice against consultants

Executives describe them as seagull consultants:
Flies in
Makes a lot of noise
Eats all the food
Craps all over everything
Flies out– never to return

Executives will derisively say, "You know you've had a visit from a seagull consultant if after the consultant has left and everything dies down, things are worse than they were before and, more important, you have wasted money using them. The seagull consultant looks impressive at first glance, but leaves disaster in their wake – and is never around to pick up the pieces. They have been paid and are gone."

Blinded by pride and excess confidence

Senior executives easily succumb to excess pride. They have confidence in themselves because of what they have created–an empire. They are often famous, wealthy, and highly paid. A pathological need for adoration, and a self-destructive need for power, prestige and notoriety, often dooms them.

Interpretation of success in one area to mean success in another

Warren Buffet was quoted in the 2004 book by James O'Loughlin, *The Real Warren Buffett: Managing Capital, Leading People*, "Apparently many managers were overexposed during impressionable childhood years in which the imprisoned, handsome prince is released from a toad's body by a kiss from a beautiful princess. Consequently, they are certain their managerial kiss will do wonders."

Belief in their own press

CEO's believe what they hear from the sycophants

surrounding them and believe they are invincible and omnipotent. They are incapable of changing direction.

Blinded by the prospect of failure

The overconfident executive vividly recalls his past actions that led to success, but is incapable to admit his past actions that resulted in failure. This executive is least likely to accept.

FIVE WAYS EXECUTIVES GO OFF TRACK

MISTAKE #1: INFORMATION OBFUSCATION

The Ivory Tower and the Powerpoint Problem

What would prevent a CEO from receiving information needed to avoid a potential catastrophe? Perhaps his direct reports don't have the courage to tell him something they know he would not like (back again to the tale of the emperor and his clothes). Or perhaps the CEO surrounds himself with subordinates who are mirror images of himself and also immune to learning what was required. It also could be that by the time the vital information reaches the executive office, it's been filtered and spun so many times that it's useless.

The CEO is dangerously remote from the real world of his business, caught in an ivory tower at least partly of his own making.

21

"Gemba is a Japanese term meaning 'the real place.' Japanese detectives call the crime scene gemba, and Japanese TV reporters may refer to themselves as reporting from gemba. In business, gemba refers to the place where value is created; in manufacturing, the gemba is the factory floor. It can be a construction site, sales floor, or where the service provider interacts directly with the customer."[1]

I took a Japanese management methods course in Tokyo. Generally speaking, Japanese companies are no more productive than American companies. However, the successful giant exporters like Toyota, Mazda, and Matsushita (Panasonic), which represent only about 15% of Japanese companies, are highly efficient and productive. At the class I attended our Instructor—Masaaki Imai—an organizational theorist and management consultant, compared the American executive style to that of the executives of elite Japanese companies. He claimed that in a Japanese company when there is a problem the executives "go to Gemba," whereas in American companies, all too often, when there's a problem the executives all go to the conference room to proclaim, "It's not my fault."

The Japanese management consultant Taichii Ohno had the practice of drawing a 30-inch circle with chalk on the shop floor and making his client spend some time standing within it. Then he would ask about the waste the executive sees and improvement potentials. He felt the chalk circle practice helped a person gain insight into a process in a way that talking about it in the conference room couldn't.

"You can observe a lot by just watching."(Yogi Berra)[2]

Clients who stood in the circle might see examples of waste relating to confusion, unclear information flow, inadequate or missing procedures, rush, and conspicuous safety problems.

Senior executives who sequester themselves in their ivory towers fail to gain an understanding of what goes on beneath them, and get no input from anyone other than their staff members. While working as president of one of Harman International's manufacturing facilities, I participated in our corporate custom requiring all executives to work one day a month in the factory, office, or warehouse. This not only gave us an appreciation of how difficult the work was and how fortunate we were to have these skilled employees, but it gave us an opportunity to become acquainted with employees levels below us and hear what was going on in "the Gemba." These day-long experiences of working alongside a factory worker often resulted in improved working conditions for that particular area. For example, the executive who left the day's work with sore feet from standing all day on a concrete floor might arrange for rubber padding to be added to that workplace floor. The TV reality series *Undercover Boss* features the experiences of senior executives working at the factory or office level in their own companies to investigate how their firms really work.

The problem of the CEO getting incorrect, incomplete, or confusing input could be the "quality" of his subordinate or it could be attributable to the *form* of the input.

"Louis V. Gerstner, the RJR Nabisco executive who became IBM's CEO and chairman in 1993 and turned it around, described his first meeting at the company. When he asked for a briefing on the state of the business, he was shown a series of slides using an overhead projector, the standard presentation format at that time. After the second slide, he walked to the front of the room, switched off the projector, and simply said, 'Let's talk about your business'. He felt there might be better ways to do serious analysis than reading aloud from projected lists."[3]

With Microsoft's release of PowerPoint for Windows around 1990, the use of bullet point presentations on overhead screens advanced to PowerPoint. There has been a great deal of criticism of the use of Power-Point for business management. Edward R. Tufte, in his book *The Cognitive Style of PowerPoint,* criticizes it for "unhelpfully simplistic tables and charts, and simplistic thinking—from ideas being squashed into bulleted lists; and stories with beginning, middle, and end being turned into a collection of disparate, loosely disguised points—presenting a misleading facade of the objectivity and neutrality that people associate with science, technology, and 'bullet points'."[4]

In his book Tufte describes the 2003 Space Shuttle Columbia catastrophe and how the use of PowerPoint by NASA engineers may have contributed to the disaster. The Colombia disintegrated on February 1, 2003 over Texas while reentering Earth's atmosphere. The accident that killed all seven crew members was caused by foam insulation that had broken off the external tank during launch and damaged the left wing.

NASA Mission Management became aware of the foam

strike as soon as it happened but needed to decide if it had caused serious damage. The engineers at NASA believed the foam strike did indeed cause serious damage. But despite the opinion of NASA engineers, NASA Management decided the strike did not create an unsafe condition and did not initiate an effort to attempt a repair. On January 23 *Columbia* Commander Husband and pilot McCool received a message from NASA flight director Steve Stitch about the foam strike and dismissed any concerns about entry safety.

When *Columbia* reentered the Earth's atmosphere, hot gases from the atmosphere entered into the damaged wing and destroyed the internal structure. This caused the spacecraft to become unstable and break apart.

Tufte in his book blames the decision on the way PowerPoint presented the data to Mission Management claiming that "vital engineering detail was buried in small type on a crowded slide with six bullet points, that if presented in a regular engineering white paper, might have been noticed and the disaster prevented."[5]

Richard Feynman the Nobel Prize physicist served on the NASA commission that investigated the first shuttle accident, the Challenger in 1986. He commented then on the bullet-outline format: "When we learned about 'bullets'—little black circles in front of phrases that were supposed to summarize things. There was one after another of these little goddamn bullets in our briefing books and on slides." [6]

Getting the right information—useful, unfiltered— from the right sources—employees at work in "the real place"—was the key to success for a Brazilian/Lebanese/French businessman who saved a major Japanese car manufacturer from bankruptcy.

Nissan Motors

It's common knowledge that Toyota's upscale model is Lexus, Honda's is Acura and Nissan's is Infinity. But it isn't common knowledge that Nissan is now a French company under the Renault name.

As Ford is America's second largest car manufacturer after GM, Nissan is Japan's second largest after Toyota. The story of Henry Ford creating his company and inventing the modern assembly line is a familiar one, but not too many people know the Nissan story. The company was founded in Yokohama in 1933 by Yoshisuke Ayukawa with engineering provided by William R. Gorham, an American expatriate. Gorham, a mechanical engineer, is considered the founder of Nissan Motor Company *in terms of technology.*

1933 Nissan (Datsun at the time). The DAT Motorcar Company was formed in 1925 and produced passenger cars under the name Datsun. In 1933, Nissan took control of Datsun.

1933 Ford Roadster

William Gorman was introduced to Japan as a young man when he became enthralled with the country and their culture. His father was a manager at B.F. Goodrich in Japan and would sometimes bring his son to visit there. After graduating as an engineer from Heald College in San Francisco, he and his father started Gorham Engineering in 1911. They designed and manufactured engines, pumps and motorboats.

The company was not successful. Frustrated with his failure in the U.S., he decided to try to get a job in Japan. The Japanese government was hiring engineers to design fighter planes for their participation in World War I on the side of the allies. In 1918, he answered an ad in a Japanese publication and took his wife and two sons to live in Japan. When he arrived, he learned the war was over and Japan no longer needed planes. He didn't have the money to travel back to the States, his family enjoyed Japan, so he decided to start a Japanese company making airplanes. That venture failed, but his next one was very successful producing a three-wheel motorized rickshaw that became very popular throughout Southeast Asia. He was considered a genius inventor in Japan and introduced his next product – an automobile. It was called the Gorham Shiki. It was a very simple car powered by a motorcycle engine. Only 60 of them were sold but he was unable to expand his company to produce in higher quantities.

During that period, he was designing boat and farm equipment engines for a close friend — Ayukara — who wanted to manufacture a car like the Model T in Japan. Both Gorham and Ayukara realized they would need a lot of equipment and talented engineers to kick off a company like that. There were a number of American car companies at that time that had failed and had equipment available for sale as well as accessible talented engineers. Gorham was able to travel to America to hire automotive engineers to move to Japan to teach the Japanese how to design and manufacture cars. He was also able to purchase a complete automobile factory from a failed car company that he shipped to Japan. Within one year, in 1933, the factory was up and running and producing the Datsun. It was the first Japanese automobile factory producing a car designed by William Gorham and the birth of Nissan. Gorham had become a Japanese hero.

By the mid-1930s the Japanese government was taken over by the military who was more interested in military vehicles than passenger cars. As World War II approached, Japan began deporting foreigners. Gorham and his wife were reluctant to leave their Japanese life and Japanese friends. They decided to renounce their U.S. citizenship and become Japanese citizens. Since Ayukara guaranteed their safety, when the Gorhams were put under house arrest after Pearl Harbor, they were very well treated.

Although Gorham spent the War designing Japanese military airplanes for Hitachi Corporation, when the U.S. government occupied Japan, they did not charge him with treason since he became a Japanese citizen before the war broke out. Douglas MacArthur, the Supreme Allied Commander, hired Gorham when he recognized how useful he could be with the U.S. effort to rebuild Japan's manufacturing capacity that had been shattered by allied bombing.

In 1951, when the Korean war broke out America was unable to produce the military hardware needed since most of those factories were converted back to producing consumer goods that were in high demand as they were not available during the war. America needed Japan's new factories to manufacture Jeeps and trucks for the American forces in the Korean War. Gorham helped Nissan produce those vehicles from 1950 to 1953.

After the war, Nissan realized they didn't have the experience to start a serious car company and signed a deal with Austin Motors in England to assemble 2000 Austin Ruby's from parts sent to Japan and sell them in Japan under the Austin name. By 1955 they had enough experience producing Austins to develop their own engines, all of which were judged as superior to Austin's.

By 1967, Nissan developed their version of an engine similar to a Mercedes design. This "L" engine was used to power the Datsun 510 that became popular throughout the world. Then in 1969, Nissan introduced the successful 240Z sports car giving Nissan world-class status.

The Nissan S30 was sold in Japan as the Nissan Fairlady Z and in America as the 240Z. The 240Z was considered by some as one of the greatest sports cars ever made.

Nissan automobiles rapidly gained worldwide popularity. They established factories in the U.S., England, Greece, Brazil, China, Spain, South Korea, India and Australia. Sales over the 27-year period from 1972 to 1999, however, were declining. The company was $27 billion in debt and needed to be rescued. Nissan allowed Renault to purchase 38% of their company. The French quickly realized that Nissan's CEO at the time —Yoshikazu Hanawa — had to be replaced and sent Carlos Ghosn, Renault's president, to Japan to become the CEO.

Carlos' Lebanese grandfather emigrated to Brazil. His son Jorge Ghosn married a Lebanese woman born in Nigeria. Carlos was born in 1954. He and his parents moved to Lebanon when he was 6 years old. He was educated in Paris with degrees in engineering and a mastery of four languages. His first job was with Michelin, Europe's largest tire company. He was promoted to Chief Operating Officer of Michelin's South American operation at age 30. He was then promoted to CEO of Michelin North America where he restructured the company and amalgamated the newly acquired Uniroyal Goodrich Tire Company. In 1996, Renault, the ailing French car company, recruited Ghosn as Executive Vice President charged with restructuring the company. His restructuring was radical. He returned Renault to profitability in one year.

Ghosn joined Nissan as COO in 1999 while he was still COO of Renault. In 2001 Ghosn announced a plan to return to profitability in 2000, achieve a profit margin of 4.5% by the end of fiscal 2002, and a 50% reduction in debt by fiscal 2002. He promised to resign if these goals were not met. "In Ghosn's speech at the Automotive News World Congress in January 11, 2012 he said, "When I launched the Nissan Revival Plan, I vowed to quit if I didn't meet all the goals I had set. The entire top management team would also leave. In the years that followed, many employees told me this gesture made all the difference. Leaders must ENGAGE AND COMMIT WHOLEHEARTEDLY. Employees will work hard if they know top management is fully committed. Employees will help you create a plan and achieve it – but only if you are in it with them." Ghosn's plan succeeded. Nissan's profits hit $2.7 billion for fiscal 2000 from a consolidated loss of $6.46 billion the year before. Only one year into his 3-year turnaround plan, Nissan had returned to profitability and within three years was one of the industry's most profitable car companies with profit margins above 9%, twice the industry average."[7]

Ghosn's career escalated; in 2008, Ghosn was named CEO of Nissan and then in 2009 was also named CEO of Renault. While Ghosn was Nissan's CEO in Japan and CEO of Renault in France, he was once again promoted in 2016. This time to Chairman of Mitsubishi Motors, recently acquired by Nissan.

Carlos Ghosn saved Nissan from collapse and transformed the company into one of the world's most profitable companies.

Ghosn's turnaround plan of Nissan was remarkable. He was quoted in an interview at the Stanford Graduate School of Business: "The best way to look for a solution is to interview as many people as possible, particularly people in critical process areas. Let me go see the people who are in charge of the process or around this process, interview them and ask, 'What's wrong? What do you think is wrong? How can you fix it?'" Ghosn interviewed hundreds of people in Nissan in order to formulate his turnaround plan. He identified purchasing and overcapacity as Nissan's key weaknesses.

Ghosn believed in committing to specific results. "When you know that a turnaround effort means changing ingrained habits, the boss needs to be frank and say it. You need to explain why you're doing it and in particular you need to commit to the results. People don't like change unless that commitment is there, if it is they may give you the benefit of the doubt and that's exactly what happened in the case of Nissan."

"Ghosn needed a plan that defied conventional wisdom, a plan that would have been unthought-of by his Japanese predecessors. Conventional norms in Japan demanded: You cannot shut down plants. You cannot challenge the seniority-based and aged-based promotion system. You cannot put younger people in charge. You cannot eliminate guaranteed lifetime employment. Nissan executives simply could not see that the unique Japanese conventions that had catapulted them to great success were the conventions that were destroying them. Yoshikazu Hanawa, Nissan's CEO at that time, was probably surrounded by subordinates who were mirror images of himself and they also were immune to seeing the cause of their failures and knowing what was required.

"Ghosn resolved the overcapacity problem by shutting down five Japanese plants, eliminating 21,000 Nissan jobs (14% of the workforce). He solved the purchasing problem by pruning his supply chain, ending ties with suppliers who were entangled with corporate buyers and their personal relationships (a system known in

Japan as keiretsu). Ghosn discovered that 25% of Nissan's steel came from just one supplier. He lowered it to 9%, an unheard-of practice in Japan.

"Nissan in 2016 under Ghosn is the sixth largest automaker in the world behind Toyota, GM, Volkswagen group, Hyundai, and Ford. The Renault-Nissan alliance is the world's fourth largest automaker. Nissan remains the leading Japanese brand in China, Russia, and Mexico." [8]

MISTAKE #2: THE YES-MEN WHO WON'T TELL THE EMPEROR HE'S NAKED

Our nation's two greatest presidents, Washington and Lincoln, were careful to assemble cabinets representing diverse viewpoints.

At the founding of our country, men like Benjamin Franklin, John Adams, Thomas Jefferson, and Alexander Hamilton were probably among the most intelligent, highly educated, well-traveled men on Earth. George Washington, although an outstanding general and excellent administrator, was neither particularly well-educated nor brilliant. His two most exceptional cabinet members were Hamilton and Jefferson, who remained bitter enemies throughout the administration. The two men traded blows in the press, with Jefferson organizing others to attack Hamilton. Hamilton responded with his own anonymous essays. Washington found it hard to understand the bitterness festering between Hamilton and Jefferson, but valued their contributions to his cabinet.

Pulitzer Prize winning author Doris Kearns Goodwin, in her book, *Team of Rivals: The Political Genius of Abraham Lincoln*, describes Abraham Lincoln's relationship with his cabinet. When Lincoln won the 1860 presidential election, he appointed to his cabinet three men who'd viciously attacked him while competing against him for the Republican presidential nomination. They were New York Sen. William H. Seward, Ohio Gov. Salmon P. Chase, and Missouri's distinguished elder statesman Edward Bates. Despite bitter personal feelings, he wanted a cabinet to help the country through the crisis of the Civil War. He didn't need yes-men. He was a political genius and brilliant administrator who knew that anyone is capable of agreeing with themselves.

A good potential root cause of information not reaching the CEO is the composition of his team, and this involves the recruiting process itself. The typical method includes developing a job profile of what qualities the successful candidate should possess in terms of technical skills and behaviors. This information is usually gleaned from other employees in the organization who are successful in similar roles. Testing then matches candidates to the success profile. Most of these tests are variants of the Myers–Briggs Type Indicator (MBTI) assessment test introduced in the 1960s, in which a psychometric questionnaire is used to measure psychological preferences in how people perceive the world and make decisions, and to explore a candidate's suitability for particular roles in management, sales, service, and technical work.

Such methods do not help the CEO assure that he will not hire just another yes-man. Nor do they guarantee that a particular candidate is a perfect fit. The senior executive who helps get a company up to $100 million in sales might not be able to bring the company up to the next level beyond $100 million. Similarly, the senior executive who is excellent at maintaining a company's stability might fail at introducing ambitious improvement initiatives. He might have that plaque on his desk that reads, *"100 Years of tradition unmarred by progress."* The corollary, of course, is that the executive who is interested in continuous improvement might be incapable and very unhappy with a job requiring maintenance of the status quo.

The challenge of recruiting a capable staff member for the CEO is different from the challenge of recruiting a capable staff member who won't be a yes-man—who could stand up to the CEO. Who would tell *the emperor he has no clothes*. Who is able to say, "no!"

Some executive recruiters excel at finding candidates who are less likely to be yes-men. These headhunters do not rely on Myers Briggs-type testing, but rather employ *behavioral interviews* to assess attitudes and patterns of behavior. One objective is to understand how willing the candidate is to challenge the CEO. The Behavioral Interview typically takes three hours.

It explores the individual's qualities related to intellect (ability to multitask, analytical skills, judgment, intuition, ability to navigate through ambiguity), personality (ability to handle pressure, conflict resolution skills, need for direction, work ethic, assertiveness), interpersonal skills (social style, networking, communication, insight), and management skills (approachability, clear expectations, team building, delegation, giving feedback).

A skilled senior executive recruiter can learn a lot about a candidate through the relatively informal, conversational approach of the Behavioral Interview. He can determine who is unlikely to simply be a yes-man. Of course, it's also the case that an occasional CEO will engage a search firm to find a subordinate who will challenge him, hire that individual, then discover he doesn't like being challenged after all. The newly hired spurned executive then joins the ranks of other, perhaps equally frustrated team members, or leaves for happier possibilities elsewhere.

Growing up, I used to watch *The Lone Ranger* on television and at the movie theater. Although *The Lone Ranger* was my favorite show, I realize now that the show's message may have poisoned corporate culture and our view of heroes.

The show started with their stirring theme music — Rossini's "William Tell Overture"—followed by a breathless announcement about a "a fiery horse with the speed of light, a cloud of dust, and hearty 'Hi-Yo, Silver!' The Lone Ranger! With his faithful Indian companion, Tonto, the daring and resourceful masked rider of the plains, led the fight for law and order in the early West. Return with us now to those thrilling days of yesteryear. The Lone Ranger rides again!" [9]

According to the fictional story, an entire patrol of Texas Rangers is massacred, except for one—the "lone" survivor. From then on, he disguises himself with a black mask and travels with Tonto, his trusty American Indian who nursed him back to health. Together, they travel across the Old West to defend helpless victims. A silver mine supplies the Lone Ranger with the name of his horse as well as the funds and bullets required to finance his wandering lifestyle.

The Lone Ranger was always centered on that same theme: helpless victims. Grandpa is living with his granddaughter, and the rustlers are stealing their cattle. The widow is living with her son, and the bank plans to foreclose on the mortgage and throw them out into the cold prairie. Perhaps Grandma is living with her grandson, and the railroad company decides to run the railroad tracks right through their living room. In every episode, these two people had something in common besides being helpless victims: they appeared stupid in their total reliance on the heroics of the Lone Ranger.

The Lone Ranger and Tonto ride into town. The Lone Ranger, it is immediately apparent, has mystic qualities. He also has two pearl-handled six shooters, a belt filled with silver bullets, and a magnificent super-horse named Silver.

The Lone Ranger quickly sizes up the situation, outwits the culprits, and rides off into the sunset, singing "Hi-Yo, Silver—away!"

As the Lone Ranger and Tonto ride off into the sunset with the townsfolk watching, somebody in the crowd asks, "Who was that masked man?" A chorus of voices reply, "That was the Lone Ranger!" And off they disappear, once again accompanied by the "William Tell Overture."

But what happens next? The new culprits come into town to cause new problems. The culprits are told by the townsfolk, "You'll be very sorry you came to our town. We have the Lone Ranger."

Sorry, folks, you don't have the Lone Ranger. The Lone Ranger is off helping other helpless victims. He isn't ever coming back to your town.

Legends like the Lone Ranger reinforce the message that we are all helpless victims who can only be helped by heroes. And that's the way it often is in the corporate suites. The staff has long given up attempts to solve problems on their own and just sit back and wait for the CEO's next (hopefully successful) heroic rescue attempt.

The Lone Ranger mirrors the culture of those flawed companies run by narcissistic CEOs desperate for adoration and recognition. They're incapable of delegating any power to their staff, who have come to regard themselves as helpless victims.

These are the all-flash-and-no-substance CEOs who often wait until the problem is at its breaking point to swoop in and save the day, Lone Ranger-style, rather than preventing it in the first place. These are the CEOs who often take credit for something that required the efforts and talents of many.

When major corporations fail, it's often due to a pervasive Lone Ranger mentality that extends all the way from the CEO down to the lower-level employees.

MISTAKE #3: POWER CORRUPTION AND FEELING INVINCIBLE

In 1973 the U.S. Office of Naval Research funded research to find out if brutality against prisoners by guards was caused by the guard's sadistic personalities or were the result of the prison environment. They were interested in brutal military guards in Navy and Marine Corps prisons. The experiment was conducted at Stanford University during August 14-20, 1973 by psychologist Philip Zimbardo.

Twenty-one male college students were selected from 75 who had responded to an ad Zimbardo put in a local newspaper looking for volunteer to play the role of either guards or prisoners for two weeks. They all had no psychological issues, no criminal history and no medical conditions. They were to be paid $15 a day to participate.

A coin flip was used to randomly determine who would be a prisoner or guard. To make it look realistic, the "suspects" selected to be prisoners were arrested at their homes by Palo Alto police officers. At their arrest, they were charged with Armed Robbery and Burglary, read their Miranda Rights, searched and handcuffed before being taken away in a police car with sirens wailing. Can you just picture the neighbors watching this?

In the meantime, the "guards" were outfitted with authentic-looking uniforms, whistles, police billy clubs and handcuffs. They were required to wear mirror sunglasses to minimize eye-contact with the prisoners. The guards were prohibited from any physical violence. Zimbardo observed the prisoners while acting as the prison superintendent and his research assistant became the warden.

The prisoners were driven to the Palo Alto police station where they received the same treatment any criminal would get. They were "booked" after having their mug shots made and fingerprinted. At this point, now in a complete state of shock, they were driven by the police to jail for more processing. The jail — Stanford County Jail — was the basement of the Stanford psychology building Zimbardo constructed to look like an authentic jail. There were no windows, bare walls and very small cells.

Upon arrival, their personal possessions were confiscated. After being stripped naked they were deloused. Bedding and uniforms were issued after which they were referred to only by an assigned number and could only refer to themselves and the other prisoners by number. Zimbardo's objective was to remove their individuality. The uniforms consisted of an uncomfortable smock with their prison number on it. They had no underwear, one ankle was chained and they had to wear a skin-tight nylon cap to make it look like their head was shaved.

Each guard was assigned nine prisoners and worked eight-hour shifts. There were three shifts. It wasn't long before guards and prisoners began behaving according to their roles. The guards started to harass prisoners and appeared to enjoy being brutal and sadistic. The guards insulted the prisoners and assigned them boring, pointless activities. The prisoners started acting like prisoners by complaining and squealing on each other to the guards. They were careful to obey all prison "rules" and often took the side of the guards against prisoners who did not. It was if they thought disobedience would be bad for all the prisoners. Cruelty by the guards increased as the prisoners became more submissive. Push-ups were a common form of physical punishment imposed by the guards. Guards stood on the prisoners' backs while they did push-ups, or would make other prisoners sit on the backs of fellow prisoners doing their push-ups. As the guards became more aggressive, demanding more respect, the prisoners grew more submissive. Guards held the prisoners in contempt and let the prisoners know it. The prisoners unquestionably respected the guards and never complained about their harsh treatment.

The experiment began to fall apart after 36 hours when one prisoner had to be released for uncontrollable rage, crying and screaming. He was diagnosed as entering a deep depression. Three other prisoners had to leave in the next few days for similar emotional problems. All these volunteers were judged to be normal and stable a few days before.

Zimbardo shut the experiment down on the sixth day. He had planned to run it for two weeks. His conclusion of the experiment was that, "people will readily conform to the social roles they are expected to play, especially if the roles are as strongly stereotyped as those of the prison guards. The *prison* environment was an important factor in creating the guards' brutal behavior (none of the participants who acted as guards showed sadistic tendencies before the study). Therefore, the findings support the situational explanation of behavior rather than the dispositional one. Only a few people were able to resist the situational temptations to yield to power and dominance while maintaining some semblance of morality and decency." [10]

I've included this prison experiment in a leadership book because the conclusion suggests that CEO's like the guards will often conform to the role they are expected to play. In the experiment, the guards or prisoners were selected randomly but their personalities were overtaken by the position of authority or submission. Perhaps the CEO who has complete control over their staff's priorities, prerogatives and careers can be compared to the guards with their overwhelming authority.

After the experiment Zimbardo shifted the focus of his work and focused on educating others about the psychology of authority and the abuse of power. He continued to lecture on the subject around the world. In 2011, he published his book *The Lucifer Effect. Understanding How Good People Turn Evil.*

Tower Records

Tom Hank's son, Colin produced the documentary film *All Things Must Pass* in 2015 about the rise and eventual fall of Tower Records. The company grew into an international brand from a modest startup in a Sacramento shop next to a drug store in the 1950's. The film features interviews with Russ Solomon –Tower's founder, as well as rock stars who were Tower shop regulars like Elton John and Bruce Springsteen who describe Tower's fantastic growth during the music boom days in the sixties through the eighties. They also describe Tower's unfortunate self-destruction and bankruptcy in the United Sates in 2006. The film shows the Tower Records shop in Tokyo that still does well and is a thriving tourist destination.

Unlike Solomon who failed, Richard Branson started a London store in 1970 called Virgin Records and Tapes in a shop above a shoe store. He provided beanbag chairs and free snacks for customers listening to music. Branson's company expanded in 1973 into Virgin Records — a recording company that he sold for $1 billion in 1992 to EMI. He used that capital in 1984 to form Virgin Airlines. One year later he began the Virgin Group that in addition to his airline, includes Virgin Mobile Phones, Virgin Books, Virgin Health Bank, Virgin Hotels, Virgin Rail Group, Virgin Cruise Lines and 400 companies in 30 countries. His net worth in 2017 was $5 billion. He's richer than the Queen (who in 2000 knighted him "Sir Richard Branson" in Buckingham Castle). Russ Solomon, however, chose to ignore many warning signs that Tower Records was heading off the roadway.

Tower Records was started by Russell Solomon in 1960 in a Sacramento building he shared with the Tower Theater. He would buy used 78 RPM vinyl records for three cents and sold them for ten cents. In time, he began selling CD's, cassettes and DVD's. Initially,

Tower expanded to Nashville, New York, Portland and Seattle. By 1999 there were 200 Tower shops in 30 countries on five continents doing over $1 billion in sales. Elton John was a regular customer buying multiple copies for all his homes. He bragged that he spent more there than anyone. John Lennon made a TV commercial for Tower.

So how did it all fall apart? The downfall began in 1998 with an uncontrolled expansion. But that was just the start. Tower Records paid a $3 million fine for price fixing in 2002 during the period 1995 – 2000. Customers were overcharged over $500 million or about $5 per album. But it was his failure to deal with his competition that brought him down. Tower began facing serious competition when Walmart and Target starting selling CD's cheaper than Tower. Tower's other threat was Solomon's stubborn refusal to reduce the price of his CD's. Just as Kodak would not accept the fact that digital photography was coming, Solomon did not believe streamed digital music was an unescapable force. Although Napster and iTunes were already doing well, in 1994 Solomon said in a promotional video that it would take a long time for people to want to have music beamed into their homes and that he will deal with it when and if it really happens. He simply didn't believe anyone would give up their CD collection. He believed people payed $18 for a CD because they wanted a physical thing for their CD collection.

That was despite the fact that Harman International and Sony had discontinued the development of CD players.

By 2004 Tower Record's debt was about $100 million with assets of just over $100 million. They could no longer fund the loans for their aggressive expansion. Tower Records filed for bankruptcy in 2006. The chain was bought for $134 million by a liquidation company who closed all the stores including the iconic, famous flagship Tower Records store on Sunset Strip in Los Angeles and liquidated the inventory. Tower's famous flagship store on London's Piccadilly Circus was bought by Richard Branson in 2003.

It would have been hard to imagine in the year 2000 that the ease of downloading books onto Kindle would destroy Borders Books and the thousands of independent book shops. Who would have thought that streamed music would end the lives of Tower Records and thousands of independent record shops? Streamed music wasn't the only problem, of course. Tower Records involvement with price fixing, its reckless expansion, the pricing policy against Walmart and Target, and loose financial management all led to the downward slide. Yet another story of "Power Corruption and Feeling Invincible" by executive management unwilling to see early warning signs and unwilling to take advice.

The Tower Records store on the Sunset Strip in Hollywood as it looked in its final year. The shop was taken over by Gibson Guitars.

MISTAKE #4: LOSS AVERSION, THE PAIN OF LOSS TRUMPS THE PLEASURE OF GAIN

The Goose That Laid the Golden Egg—an Aesop fable.

"ONE day a countryman going to the nest of his Goose found there an egg all yellow and glittering. When he took it up it was as heavy as lead and he was going to throw it away, because he thought a trick had been played upon him. But he took it home on second thoughts, and soon found to his delight that it was an egg of pure gold. Every morning the same thing occurred, and he soon became rich by selling his eggs.

As he grew rich he grew greedy; and thinking to get at once all the gold the Goose could give, he killed it and opened it only to find,—nothing."

"Kill the goose that lays the golden eggs" is a fanciful way of saying "seek short-term gain at the sacrifice of long-term profit." The fable also illustrates "loss aversion." Kodak had its chemical and print business in hand and was risk averse about losing it—even if the digital camera business was better. People don't like giving up stuff.

In the documentary film *The Armstrong Lie*, racer Lance Armstrong explains what drives him:

"I like to win, but more than anything, I can't stand this idea of losing. Because to me, losing means death." After years of denials, Armstrong admitted doping in January 2013, and was stripped of all seven of his victories in the Tour de France in 2012.

Daniel Kahneman, an Israeli-American psychologist famous for his work on the psychology of judgment and decision-making, was awarded the 2002 Nobel Memorial Prize in Economic Sciences for his work on loss aversion.

"In economics and decision theory, loss aversion refers to people's tendency to strongly prefer avoiding losses to acquiring gains. Most studies suggest that losses are twice as powerful, psychologically, as gains. Once you have put time or money into a company, you are willing to take irrational risks to protect your investment. It's like the person who invested in a stock that is worth less than he paid and is continuing to go down. He can't bear the thought of selling at a loss and admitting failure so he irrationally holds onto it until his stock tanks."[11]

The lesson from this is that the CEO must be cautious of the human inclination to avoid loss, even if it means taking reckless risk. This suggests he must carefully consider the suitability of those people around him who he may seek for council.

These examples of stubborn CEO's I've cited implies their stubbornness is a trait of CEO's. But it might be that the situation of being a CEO takes a "normal person" and makes them a "different person."

Lego

The following is an inspirational story about how Lego, on the verge of bankruptcy in 2003, was *saved* by the founder's grandson who stepped aside as CEO and put his faith in an outsider.

The Lego group originated in the carpentry shop of Ole Kirk Christiansen in Billund, Denmark, where he made ladders and ironing boards. In 1932, as a result of Denmark's depression at the time, Christiansen couldn't get the materials he needed, so he collected scraps of wood to begin making toys for kids. His wood duck turned out to be a big hit and he converted his business into toy making. He named his company "Lego," a derivative of the Danish phrase *leg godt* that means "play well." In 1947, Lego began producing plastic toys and in 1949, an early version of what we now recognize as the bricks with interlocking studs and tubes.

In 1954, Christiansen's son Godtfred replaced his father as head of the company–The Lego Group. He had a vision that Lego bricks could become *a system for creative play*. When you buy a second Lego set, it's not just an additional toy; since the bricks interlock, the new set allows the child to multiply what's possible to build. With more sets, more opportunities. Pieces from different sets can be combined. The pieces from the castle will fit into the space station.

Godtfred recognized initially that the bricks had technical problems. They didn't lock well and weren't sufficiently versatile. The current brick's look took until 1958 to develop and patent, then another five years to find the right material, ABS polymer. This was important because Lego pieces are assembled and disassembled many times and must not wear out or stop holding together.

Take a look at the photo of the Lego bricks. Doesn't it look like an easy thing to design and manufacture? It actually is a highly complex product. The molding machines that make the bricks hold tolerances of 1/10 the thickness of a human hair. Bricks made in 1958 still interlock with bricks made today. Lego bricks must not only snap together and hold firmly, they must be easy to take apart. The design is quite clever – six Lego bricks can be combined in 900 million ways.

In 1979, after 25 years of success, Godtfred Christiansen, who in 1979 turned the company's management over to Lego's third Christiansen leader — his son, Kirk.

Lego's popularity spread throughout Europe where three Legoland Parks were built. But Lego hit the wall in the 1993-1998 period. Lego had their first financial loss resulting in the elimination of 1000 jobs. The company was in serious trouble. Their strategy during that period was to introduce many more new models but the market showed no interest in them. Many of the new models had features like electric motors and fiber optics. But their financial management systems were weak – they had no idea how much it cost to make their products or how much profit, if any, the different products made. They eventually learned the products with the features like motors and optics cost more to make than they sold for.

Much of their problems was caused by a decision to replace the designers who created the successful products of the 70's, 80's and 90's with top graduates of the best design colleges in Europe. These new people may have been superb designers, but they knew little about designing toys and nothing about building with Lego sets. One of their failed products was a castle set that needed to be held together with Crazy Glue after assembly to keep it from toppling over. That, of course, defeats the fun of Lego sets that can be built and then taken apart to build something new. Customers found some of the new Lego sets to be too easy to build. Kids like to be challenged.

During this misguided period of accelerated innovation and new product introduction, the number of parts produced quickly climbed from 6,000 to 12,000 and the number of colors increased from six to fifty, causing tremendous logistics problems and skyrocketing manufacturing costs. Despite a 17% increase in sales, there was no increase in profits. Many of the new innovative products were good, but only six percent were making money. Simply stated, Lego had too many products and not enough profits.

By 2003, Lego was near collapse. Major retailers like Walmart and Target were stuck with unsold Lego sets from Christmas of 2002. Analysts were predicting construction type toys would never appeal to kids enthralled with video games. The only thing keeping the company solvent at that point was the wealth of the private founding family. Lego started selling off assets, including 70% of the four Legoland parks for $187 million to Merlin Entertainment who owned the London Eye and Madame Tussauds.

In 2001, the nose-diving Lego Group hired 33-year-old Jorge Vig Knudstorp, a former McKinsey consultant, to take charge of their eight-person strategic development department. By 2004 he completely understood the company's situation and created a plan to save the company. That same year, Lego's CEO, Kjeld Kirk Christensen, the grandson of Lego's founder, gave up his position and put Knudstorp in charge. Christensen remained chairman of the board.

Knudstorp took charge quickly. He made extensive staff reductions, reduced the number of parts to 6,000, analyzed all costs and made the necessary changes to selling prices, shut down the Lego computer game business, and most importantly, removed creative control from designers who never played with Legos. New design managers were put in place who were already working in the company, loved the product, knew the customers, grew up playing with Legos, and were bursting with ideas they had been sitting on for years.

Knudtorp's efforts were remarkable. By the end of 2005, Lego went from a $292 million loss to a pre-tax profit of $117 million. Sales that year hit $1.2 billion and profits tripled. "By 2014, Lego had overtaken Mattel to become the world's largest and most profitable toy company and Legos are the most popular toy of all time. These volumes are staggering. Seven Lego sets are sold every second someplace on earth. 500 bricks per second are produced, which represents 22 billion plastic bricks per year. Lego is the number one manufacturer of automobile tires, even though those are the tiny tires made for Lego vehicles." [12]

Knudstorp's long-term goal was to achieve growth

by leading his executive team away from a focus on growth. He believed the growth would happen naturally if the company leadership stuck to basic management principles. In an interview in 2004 in answer to the question, "What leadership approach did you apply to pull Lego back from the brink?" he replied:

"When I became CEO, things had gone awfully wrong at Lego Group. To survive the company needed to halt a sales decline, reduce debt and focus on cash flow. It was a classic turnaround and I required tight steady control and top-down management. At the same time, I had to build credibility. You can make a lot of things happen if you are viewed without suspicion, so I made sure I was approachable. In Danish, we have an expression that literally translates as, 'managing at eye level,' but it means being able to talk to people on the factory floor, to engineers, to marketers–being at home with everyone.

"Once the company had gained the freedom to live and have a strategy, the management team set out to optimize the firm's value. In order to do that, we had to ask, 'Why does Lego Group exist?' Ultimately, we determined the answer: to offer our core products whose unique designs help children learn systematic, creative problem solving — a crucial twenty-first century skill. We decided we wanted to compete — not by being the biggest but by being the best. Implementing a strategy of niche differentiation and excellence requires a looser structure and a relaxation of the top-down management style we had imposed during the turnaround because the company needed empowered managers.

"Now we're in a third phase—to continue building sales volume, we need to change the leadership style again because the company's management had become quite risk averse while focusing on survival. Now we need to become opportunity driven, which requires taking greater calculated risks. We have been paving the way by moving managers within the corporation and altering organizational structures and ways of working.

"The way I manage my team is like an orchestra conductor. There's a bunch of virtuosos and high performing individuals in the orchestra. I will never tell them how to play the violin. But I will tell them if they're not playing the same score as the rest of the orchestra."[13]

The hero of the Lego story isn't Knudstorp. Kirk Christensen, who would not succumb to loss aversion, who hired Knudson, is the hero. He understood he couldn't save Lego and needed to put his trust in an outsider. Otherwise Lego would be on the same list a Kodak and Tower Records.

Polaroid

Who would have guessed in 1960 that digital photography would put an end to the snapshot? It would have been hard to imagine that the digital slide show would replace the photo album.

Edwin Herbert Land, an American scientist and inventor best known for founding the Polaroid Corporation, was second only to Thomas Edison in the number of patents he received. Just as it is surprising that the stubbornness of a genius like Edison led to the demise of his electrical power distribution company, we have a similar story with Edwin Land. His profitable instant photography business accounted for 100% of the instant photography business, 20% of the film market, 10% of the American camera market in the 1960s, and employed 21,000 people, but went bankrupt in 2001. Polaroid's share price dropped from $140 in 1973 to $0.24 in 1991.

Edwin Land's inability to understand the threat of digital photography to Polaroid is like Tower Record's blindness to the CD, Blockbuster's blindness to Netflix, and Schwinn, which couldn't accept that mountain biking wasn't just a passing fad.

Land had the goose that would keep laying golden

eggs forever. Polaroid film had a 70% margin. Edwin Land was reluctant to abandon sales of instant film when the popularity of instant print cameras and film began to wane. He resisted expanding the production and sale of the excellent digital cameras he patented. His margins on the sale of digital cameras would be 38%. Making film was far more profitable and much easier than producing hardware.

It is amazing that the two companies who developed and held the patents on digital cameras—Kodak and Polaroid—both went bankrupt for believing their customers wanted to have prints of their photographs. Both companies could be thriving today – they had numerous opportunities to correct their downward spirals. They simply chose to ignore the evidence before their eyes, their own market research, and advice from people they should have trusted. An interesting side note: Edwin Land was the hero of Macintosh's Steve Jobs–he idolized him. We have all seen videos of Jobs introducing his new technology to his shareholders from a stage. Land had been doing that same thing thirty years earlier. In 1972, Land introduced the revolutionary new SX-70 Polaroid camera while sitting on stage on a desk chair next to a Saarinen brand tulip table. A photo of Steve Jobs introducing the iPad to shareholders shows him sitting next that exact same table.

It's clear that Steve Jobs learned a lot from Edwin Land, who in the 1960s turned shareholder meetings into dramatic presentations of his latest "coveted luxury items" sometimes accompanied by live music.

Neither man believed in market research. Land's principle was, "My job is not to ask the public what they want. My job is to give them what they can't even imagine." Steve Jobs got that from Land. Jobs commented on the Macintosh, "If I asked someone who had only used a personal calculator what a Macintosh should be like, they couldn't have told me. There was no way to do consumer research on it so I had to go and create it and then show it to people and say 'Now what do you think?'" [14]

Land and Jobs had a great deal in common. Both were college dropouts and both built companies popular with both Wall Street and Main Street. Both men were tossed out when their companies were floundering. During that time Land made the fatal mistake of squandering billions of dollars developing an instant movie camera and projector. Both products were doomed in 1975 when Sony introduced Betamax – a video tape recording and playback format. After Land left, Polaroid went broke. It was a different story with Apple. After Steve Jobs left Apple, the company continued its downhill slide. The only thing that saved it was Jobs' return and his leadership that gambled with new technology.

Edwin Herbert Land (1909-1991) was born in Connecticut, the son of a Russian-Jewish immigrant father who owned a scrap metal yard. In 1926, a Harvard student walking along Broadway in New York City, he recognized that glare from headlights and store signs could be a safety hazard. He dropped out of school to develop a polarizing light filter that could reduce the danger. He returned to Harvard where he and his teacher formed a company to produce polarizing filters for Kodak. They called their company Polaroid. Their initial products were for cameras and sunglasses, but they prospered as a defense contractor in World War II when they developed military applications of their technology, including missile guidance lenses, dark-adaptation goggles, and stereoscopic viewing systems to reveal camouflaged enemy positions in aerial photography.

Land's idea for the instant camera came to him in 1947 while on vacation in Santa Fe with his 3-year old daughter, who asked why she couldn't see a photograph he took of her right away. The camera he developed was a hit from the moment it was introduced before the 1948 Christmas holidays. For the next two decades, the Polaroid camera became widely used, not only for photo albums, but for business applications like driver's licenses, crime reports, insurance investigations, and real estate ads.

By 1974, Polaroid estimated that 1 billion instant photographs were taken that year. But the digital revolution was coming and Polaroid's attempts to prepare themselves for it were inadequate. They began a digital imaging group. By 1989, 42% of Polaroid's R&D was being spent on digital imaging and by the late 1990s, Polaroid for a brief period was a top seller of digital cameras. But Land stubbornly refused to promote them adequately.

The digital revolution was bringing changes that hurt many traditional businesses unexpectedly.

Newspapers lost classified advertising and subscribers. Network TV viewers started watching cable and Web sites, which eliminated commercials. The recording industry radically changed when music could be downloaded for free.

In the 1970s, the digital minilab—a small photographic developing and printing system—replaced large centralized photo developing labs. This allowed retailers to offer on-site photo finishing services.

In addition to being hurt by the digital revolution, Polaroid suffered from customers discovering that 35 mm color film was cheaper, easier to use, and made better quality prints than instant film. That problem was compounded by new competition—the proliferation of one-hour photo processing.

Polaroid was unable to follow through on its development of Polaroid digital cameras and unable to adjust to the new market realities. One of their catastrophic market assumptions was that customers would always need an instantly available high quality paper print.

In his 1985 letter to shareholders, McAllister Booth, Polaroid's CEO, wrote, "As electronic imaging becomes more prevalent, there remains a basic human need for a permanent visual record." Land's mistaken beliefs and prejudices had become institutionalized. Throughout the 1990s, Polaroid executives continued to believe in the need for the paper print. Gary DiCamillo, Polaroid's CEO from 1995 -2001, said in 2008, "People were betting on hard copy and media that was going to be pick-up-able, visible, seeable, touchable as a photograph should be." When it became very obvious that Polaroid customers abandoned print, DiCamillo said, "This was a major mistake we all made. That was a major hypothesis that I believed in my marrow was wrong." Polaroid was blind to the eventuality that the photo album would be replaced by the digital slide show.

Polaroid, like Kodak, viewed itself principally as a chemical company and desperately tried to salvage that part of their business. Polaroid should have remained focused on the digital cameras instead of doubling down on photographic chemistry research to reduce the cost of their instant film.

Another misstep was Polaroid's war with Kodak—a war that ultimately led to the destruction of both companies.

Kodak's Instant Camera

Kodak was manufacturing film for Polaroid in the early 1970s. Kodak sold their own instant camera from 1976 - 1986, using what Polaroid claimed were their patents. Polaroid sued for patent infringement and sought triple damages of $12 billion, claiming it suffered loss of market share and unfair price competition because of Kodak. But Kodak said it had only cost Polaroid $343 million and termed Polaroid's claim "excessive."

In October 1990, Polaroid Corp. won $909 million in the long-running (15 year) instant photography patent-infringement suit against Eastman Kodak Co. U.S. District Judge A. David Mazzone in Boston ruled that Polaroid had lost profits of nearly $250 million because of Kodak's illegal actions.

"But the $909-million award, which also reflects interest and royalties, was far less than the $2.5 billion some Wall Street analysts expected, or the $5.7 billion in lost profit and interest Polaroid demanded in court papers led in February 1988. This was a tremendous disappointment to Polaroid and viewed as a "negative award" by stock analysts. Experts believe this was fatal to Polaroid, not only because of the wasted time and money involved with the case, but because it was a blow to the spirit of the company." [15]

Land's attempted follow-up to the instant still camera—Polavision instant movies—was a failure in 1977. The $700 camera cost too much, could not record sound, only recorded in black and white, required very bright lights, and only exposed 2 1/2 minutes of film per cartridge. When it failed to win consumer acceptance, the company ended up writing off $68.5 million in Polavision expenses. Consumers chose a competing invention: Sony's Betamax videotape recorder.

A few years later Polaroid suffered another blow when the Japanese began marketing autofocus, auto light-adjust cameras in the United States. That development, together with proliferating one-hour photo shops, made instant still cameras virtually obsolete.

Polaroid's instant camera sales—and profit—plunged. Edwin Land was eased out of the Company by the board in July 1982. His stock holdings at that time were worth $1 billion.

Land was too obstinate to change his plan and would not listen to alternatives he was offered. Time, money, talent and resources he threw into his hopeless battle with Kodak could have been used for other projects like a Polaroid digital camera. Another possibility that could have saved Polaroid would have been a merger with Kodak.

Work on instant movies should have been abandoned. It was common knowledge that the Betamax and VCR were coming.

Polaroid had developed a line of ink cartridges for digital printers, but abandoned the business.

Today, Apple is one of the richest companies in America. Everything they attempt lately is successful. People line up in front of Apple stores to get their latest releases. It wasn't always that way. In the 1980's and 1990's not all their products were successes and the company was struggling. The company became successful with the well-received iPod in 2001. Among the products that failed prior to the iPad were the G4 Cube, TAM Computer, Pippin Video Game, iPod Wi-Fi, iPhone5C,

16-pound "portable" Macintosh TV, Hockey Puck Mouse, Apple III, and the Lisa Computer.

Apple kept trying, but the doomed leaders of Polaroid and Kodak were paralyzed.

You Gotta Know When to Fold 'em

Kenny Rogers 1978 song The Gambler is about knowing when to hold or fold.

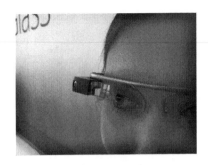

Examples of products that folded. New Coke that debuted in 1985 was "folded" in 2002. Google Glass was short-lived. Production that started in 2013 was discontinued in 2015.

Blockbuster

When Blockbuster, the movie rental company, crossed paths with Netflix, the results amounted to a David and Goliath internet streaming story.

"How Goliath, upon seeing David coming with stones, reproached him for his age and appearance and because he had come to him as one would come to a dog, with stones instead of with a sword. Yet, David answers him saying: 'you come to me trusting your arms, but I come to you trusting my God.' As he was saying this, he hastily took a stone, placed it in his sling and smote Goliath, who was drawing near to meet him, in his forehead with so much force, that the stone was affixed to Goliath's forehead and he sank to the ground. Seeing this, the terrified Philistines turned their backs and fled. David, on the other hand, approached Goliath and, as he did

not have a sword of his own, killed him with his sword and cut off his head" (I Samuel 17: 41–51).

That's the Bible story, now here's a modern-day version.

Reed Hasting, who started a DVD-by-mail service (those red envelopes), in 1998 proposed a partnership to John Antioco, CEO of Blockbuster. Blockbuster at that time had a market value of $5 billion, with millions of customers and 9,000 stores staffed by 60,000 employees. Hastings started Netflix, or so the story goes, because he was unhappy about owing a $40 late fee to Blockbuster for a copy of Apollo 13. Antioco could have accepted the partnership deal from Hastings and owned Netflix for $50 million. The Netflix company Antioco could have had in 1998 for $50 million had a market value of $33 billion (that's billion with a "B") in 2015 with 81 million customers in 190 countries.

Blockbuster did not do well after that. By 2010, Blockbuster was sold to satellite-TV company DISH Network at a bank auction for $320 million. Dish outbid the Korean company SK Telecom. In 2014, Blockbuster closed their remaining 320 stores and laid off the last 2800 employees. Carl Icahn, Blockbuster's largest shareholder, who at one point accumulated some 17 million shares of the company, in 2011 said Blockbuster was the worst investment he ever made.

The Red Envelope

So what did the Blockbuster CEO do wrong and what did the CEO of Netflix do right? Blockbuster had a good concept to begin with: you can have a DVD by just going to your nearest Blockbuster store. Just about every neighborhood had one. Netflix, on the other hand, made you wait until the DVD you wanted came in the mail. Here we have one more example of a CEO with cognitive dissonance. Of course, Antioco understood Blockbuster made a lot of money charging their customers late fees. In 2000 Blockbuster collected nearly $800 million in late fees accounting for a high percent of their total income. But he simply could not see that penalizing customers was a doomed strategy.

Netflix had certain advantages. By not having retail stores, their costs were lower than Blockbuster's and, therefore, the company could offer a greater variety. And best of all: Instead of charging to rent videos, it offered subscriptions, which made late fees unnecessary. Customers could watch a video for as long as they wanted or return it and get a new one. Eventually, Antioco realized how much of a threat Netflix was and proceeded to launch a plan that could have saved Blockbuster. The plan was to eliminate late fees, which would cost the company $200 million, and to invest $200 million to start a Blockbuster streaming video service. The board, as well as Carl Icahn, did not agree with the plan and fired Antioco in 2005. Blockbuster went bankrupt in 2010.

Netflix not only survived, they thrived mightily. In July, 2017, they reported a growth to 100 million subscribers in 190 countries.

The DVD-by-mail service they started in 1998 gave way to streaming in 2007. Netflix remains a quickly growing, nimble company acutely aware of market trends. DVD rental by mail customers have shrunk to about a quarter of total customers and that number continues to shrink as the number of streaming subscribers grow. Netflix has become the leading Internet television network, with millions of customers all over the world. Netflix places no limits on how much streaming subscribers watch. They can watch on any internet connected device anywhere and can play, pause, and resume watching. And best of all, there are no commercials.

Netflix began their business of original series with *House of Cards,* which debuted in 2013, and now produces hundreds of hours of original programming around the world. In 2015, Netflix—the David in this story—began its confrontation with their next Goliath, the Hollywood movie studios, with their first original movies. In 2016, Netflix won the right to the new film named *Bright*, a fantasy starring Will Smith. Netflix (we know as strictly an online streaming service) defeated (outbid) the giant Warner Brothers to the right for the film that could be the next big franchise similar to *Men in Black*. This could get Netflix into the real "big money" and that could happen if say, they can purchase a film like *Transformers* or *Harry Potter*.

Blockbuster's Antioco's failure to realize how quickly Netflix would grow is much like Tower Record's inability to appreciate the threat of music streaming and Schwinn's denial of the mountain bike craze (more about Schwinn later). In each case, CEOs delayed correcting for oncoming traffic until it was too late. They thought they had all the time in the world.

MISTAKE #5: LATER RATHER THAN SOONER

THE "S" CURVE AND THE ALL "THE TIME IN THE WORLD" MINDSET

There are many examples of companies whose products were made obsolete by new technology. For example:

Old Technology	New Technology
The typewriter *(Remington, Olivetti)*	Word Processor *(Apple, Dell)*
Vacuum Tubes *(Bendix, Dumont, Sylvania RCA)*	Semiconductors *(Intel, Texas Instrument, Fairchild)*
Film Cameras (Kodak, Olympus, Pentax, Yashika, Rollei)	Digital Cameras (Canon, Sony, Nikon, iPhone)
VHS Tape (RCA JVC, AMPEX)	DVD (Maxell, Sony, TDK)
Mechanical Calculators (Monroe, Burroughs, Smith Corona)	Digital Calculators (Casio, Canon, Texas Instrument)
Mechanical Wristwatch (Gruin, Elgin)	Digital Wristwatch (Casio, Timex)
Landline Telephone (Bell)	Digital Telephones (Apple, Samsung)
Printed Newspapers (*New York Daily Mirror, New York Herald Tribune, LA Herald Examiner*)	Online news (Huffington Post, Newsweek)
Printed Matter (Airline tickets, magazines, calendars, photos, phone book)	On computer, On Phone

Some of the companies whose products were made obsolete survived; others did not. Why did some make it and not others?

Product development typically follows a business cycle called an S-Curve. During the initial phase when the product is first introduced to the market, it's only used by a small group of early adopters or hobbyists. As the product improves and gets broader market appeal, the design becomes standardized and manufacturing capabilities are improved. At this point, competition becomes interested, which spurs development on product performance and production cost. This is the period of greatest growth. This is the point where it doesn't take much technology or cash to yield huge dividends. Then the curve begins to level off and plateau as the product reaches market saturation. Competition has emerged, margins are driven down, and the product is facing extinction. In his 1996 book, *Only the Paranoid Survive,* Hungarian-born American businessman, engineer, Intel founder, Andy Grove writes, "Business success contains the seeds of its own destruction. The more successful you are, the more people want a chunk of your business and then another chunk and then another until there is nothing left."

At this point, the decision needs to be made about investing more into the corporation's cash cow or diverting capital to a promising new market opportunity that may eventually displace the existing business. You don't know how long it will take for this new technology to be market viable, much less have the ROI of the existing business. Furthermore, you make the new business dependent on the old for resources, facilities, talent, etc., and the new technology is absorbed by the old and the opportunity lost. The companies who took the gamble on the new technology survived.

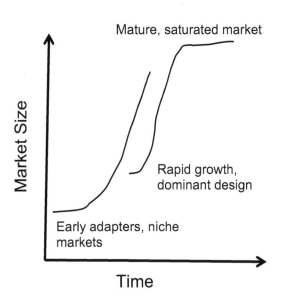

The S-Curve

A company's focus needs to be on two things: the management of the life-cycle of the existing technology and when the existing product reaches maturity to begin work on either a next-generation product or an entirely new product.

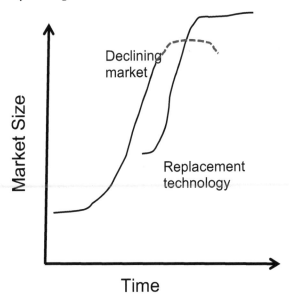

The replacement technology's S-Curve that will replace the first.

The competitive stories of Kodak and Fujifilm are telling examples.

Kodak was fully aware of the oncoming wave of digital technology. They built their own digital camera as early as 1975. Kodak senior executives had a report in 1979 projecting that the photography market would shift permanently to digital by 2010. At the beginning of this book I described my discussion with Dr. Bradley

Paxton who in 1989 as Kodak's VP and GM of their Electronic Photography Division explained their new digital camera patent to Kodak's CEO and top executives. The digital wave could not be called a surprise.

Consider this from Adrian Wooldridge in the January 2012 *Economist*:

"Like Kodak, Fujifilm realized in the 1980s that photography would be going digital. Like Kodak, it continued to milk profits from film sales, invested in digital technologies, and tried to diversify into new areas. Like Kodak, the folks in the wildly profitable film division were in control and late to admit that the film business was a lost cause. As late as 2000, Fujifilm counted on a gentle 15 to 20-year decline of film—not the sudden freefall that took place. Within a decade, film went from 60% of Fujifilm's profits to basically nothing.

If the market forecast, strategy, and internal politics were the same, why the divergent outcomes? The big difference was execution.

Fujifilm realized it needed to develop in-house expertise in the new businesses. In contrast, Kodak seemed to believe that its core strength lay in brand and marketing, and that it could simply partner or buy its way into new industries, such as drugs or chemicals. The fatal error Kodak made was their assumption of the slope of the digital camera's S–Curve. They were convinced it would take a long time for digital to catch on. Simply stated: Kodak went bankrupt by waiting too long to change."

Schwinn Bicycles

The Schwinn Black Phantom was introduced as the top of the balloon tire line. It had all the right stuff—chrome fenders and horn, fake motorcycle-style fuel tank, whitewall tires, head and tail lights, spring fork, deluxe saddle, and more. This is the bike every boy wanted.

Those "rags-to riches-to rags" stories abound about how a family business that had been profitable for decades was destroyed by the less talented third-generation senior executive.

One of the most interesting is the story of the Schwinn Bicycle Company founded in 1895 by Ignaz Schwinn and bankrupted in 1993 during the reign of Edward Schwinn, Junior, his great-grandson.

For decades, Schwinn had been the iconic, premium American bicycle and ruled the market. Schwinn bikes in the baby boom of the 50s were the envy of neighborhood kids.

Ignaz remained president until the late 40s, when he was in his 80s. His son Frank, known as F.W., ran the company though the profitable post-war 1950s. F.W. turned the management over to his son, Frank, who did little to grow or improve the company, which managed to survive based primarily on its past, but deteriorating reputation.

Andrew Grove, one of the founders and CEO of Intel Corporation, the world's largest manufacturer of semiconductors, had a motto:

Success breeds complacency
Complacency breeds failure
Only the paranoid survive

Frank's probable lack of paranoia set the downward course for the company. In 1980, the bicycles were produced in Schwinn's massive factory in Chicago employing 1400 people. The entire bike was fabricated there. Workers made every part, welded the frames, chrome plated the fenders and trim, even laced the wheels. Unfortunately, the factory had become a dinosaur. Frank did nothing to upgrade the antiquated facility. He was competing with efficient bicycle factories in Japan, Taiwan and China who had machinery that could accommodate the new lighter, stronger materials.

An employee strike for higher wages compelled Frank to shut the plant and move to Greenville, Mississippi—away from unions and where labor rates were low. The plan was to purchase components from Asia and use the Greenville plant only for assembly. The plant was a failure for a number of reasons, including an inability to get skilled workers and the distance from rail lines, headquarters, and the West Coast where the components entered the country from Asia. That plant finally closed in 1991, laying off 250 workers.

Schwinn had two opportunities for great success in the 1970s and blew both of them. They entered the popular BMX craze too late and using their existing frames, which were not nearly as good as the competition. The final blunder was their inability to take advantage of the new mountain biking phenomena starting in California. Youngsters in Marin County were searching used bike shops for 1930s-era Schwinn fat tire bikes to ride down Mount Tamalpais. Schwinn thought this was a passing fad and reluctantly entered the market with an inadequate bike they didn't even list in their catalog. But competition was entering the market and becoming very successful selling expensive mountain bikes while Schwinn persisted in their belief this was a soon-to-pass fad.

Edward Jr, — the last Schwinn — was similar to his father. He had a reputation of alienating employees, distributors and bankers he dealt with. He witnessed his company go bankrupt and have the brand name sold off to low-end bicycle producers who display their Schwinn bicycles, shorts and cycling accessories at Walmart and Target.

Frank had every right to be paranoid, but he wasn't. He should have been paranoid about the Asian factories he was competing with who could produce superior bicycles at lower costs than he could. He should have been paranoid about the labor unrest in the ancient Chicago factory that because of corporate inattention eventually led to a crippling strike. He should have been paranoid about his competitors who entered the profitable BMX market with designs and materials he could have been pursuing. He should have been paranoid about startup bike companies like Fisher and Specialized who jumped on the mountain bike craze and are still successful today (the Specialized company motto is, "Innovate or Die").

In the preface to this book, I describe how managing a company is like driving a car. The driver doesn't hold the wheel rigidly, but makes constant small corrections as the road surface and direction change. If that doesn't happen, a crash is all too likely. In business, senior management needs to constantly make corrections in the direction of the enterprise based on signals—always assuring that the path being followed is in line with the company's strategy, vision, goals, and survival. Schwinn received signals requiring course correction for decades, but chose to ignore them.

Why would Schwinn ignore warnings they received for decades that were telling them to change course?

Even in 1991 as Schwinn was being purchased at a bankruptcy auction, the family stuck to their excuse that they could not compete with the Chinese. They viewed themselves as helpless victims. That, of course, was not the case. They had ignored warning signals and continued to believe they had "all the time in the world."

The Swiss Watch

The $10 digital watch. A marvel of engineering. Accurate to within seconds per year (more accurate than a $10,000 Rolex), lightweight, shockproof, water-tight down to 100 meters, built-in useful functions, including a lighted face, a stopwatch, a timer, and an alarm.

During the 1970's the Swiss dominated 65% of the mechanical watchmaking industry. By 1988 62,000 of the 90,000 workers in the Swiss watchmaking industry lost their jobs. Companies who had produced brands that had existed for centuries shut their doors.

Who invented the digital watch? Would you believe it was the Swiss?

The $10 Digital Watch

Watchmaking has been Switzerland's most famous industry for 300 years, growing from the seventeenth century development of small mechanical clock movements. Some companies established back then are still in business today. During World War II, Swiss neutrality allowed the country to continue making watches, while other nations needed to shift their watchmaking efforts to military timing devices. By the end of the war, Switzerland had the monopoly on watchmaking—the competition was gone. Exports of Swiss pocket watches and wristwatches, from inexpensive hand wound to self-winding or automatic, had risen to 40 million units by 1973. But ten years later, that number plummeted to only three million.

Switzerland's centuries of watchmaking tradition in the early 1970s was decimated by a new technology: quartz watches. They use a battery to power a quartz crystal to vibrate at an extremely accurate and regular frequency that controls a motor which turns the watch's hands. These watches are far more accurate and cheaper than most mechanical watches. And where did this quartz watch technology come from? It came from five years of research and development at Switzerland's CEH research center established in 1962 in Neuchatel to develop a Swiss-made quartz wristwatch.

But the Swiss watchmaking industry regarded the quartz watch as a mere novelty–a fad that would quickly fade. The quartz watch only had a few parts compared with hundreds of precision parts in a mechanical watch. There was no challenge.

The Swiss viewed their mechanically excellent watches as their national identity that would guarantee their continued success and survival.

At the same time, the Japanese and Americans were about to get into the market. In 1975, Texas Instruments developed the plastic case and brought out the first LED watch at a price of $20 and that dropped to $10 the following year. Texas Instruments produced 18 million of these watches per year until 1981, when they exited the watch business. Although the revenue was high, their profits were negligible. Other American digital watch companies also pulled out of the industry, with the exception of Timex.

The Japanese became the winners of the race. They invested heavily into research and development of quartz technology. Japan had been making watches for quite a while. Seiko began production in Tokyo in 1892 and Citizen was founded in 1918. All watches produced by Seiko and Citizen were mechanical until 1960, when their work began on an electronic watch. The Japan Clock & Watch Association estimates quartz watches accounted for 98 percent of all watches produced worldwide in 2011.

The quartz watch revolution was a catastrophe for Switzerland. By 1983, not only was there a loss of thousands of jobs, there was the financial loss of the loss of millions of dollars of equipment that had to be scrapped, and the upcoming need to invest in new technology and retraining a new workforce.

The first Swatch prototype was made in 1981. Instead of the standard 91 components found in watches, the Swatch had only 51. Most important, the quartz-run plastic watches were identical in components and shape so they could be produced entirely by robots. The combination of marketing and manufacturing expertise restored Switzerland as a major player in the world market.

The Swatch Watch Company was formed by a merger of two weak companies who set out to launch Swatch watches as a relatively cheap, full branded, trendy line in 1983. Swatch desperately needed to re-capture entry level market share lost during the quartz crisis and the Japanese competitors Seiko and Citizen.

They were wildly successful They sold 2.5 million in less than two years and put Switzerland back in the wrist watch business. Swatch watches account for 18% of international watch sales.

Switzerland returned as a major of the world market

by their revolutionary manufacturing techniques and marketing expertise. They simplified the watch's movement design by reducing the number of component from 91 to 51 and developed a watch case designed with synthetic materials selected to allow the final case assembly to be ultrasonically welded. A totally automated assembly process was created in a clean-room that required no human intervention. This highly efficient manufacturing technology allowed Swatch to produce their brand economically, and enabled them to acquire many other brands including; Breguet, Harry Winston, Blancpain, Glashütte Original, Jaquet Droz, Léon Hatot, Omega, Longines, Rado, Union Glashütte, Tissot, Balmain, Certina, Mido, Hamilton, and Calvin Klein. Who knew? In addition to acquiring these firms, they also supply parts and components to the entire watchmaking industry. Swatch today is the largest watch producer in the world with 156 manufacturing centers. The Swatch name was created by the combination of the two words, "second" and "watch."

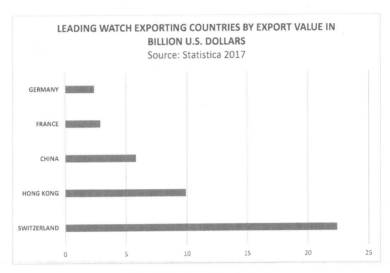

Swiss Watchmaking is back

Swiss watchmaking has certainly returned. The economic calamity created by the quartz watch in the 1970's that dropped Swiss watchmaking jobs to under 30,000 was overcome by Swatch investment and innovation. Today the Swiss watch industry employs 57,000 people in 500 companies. If you combine jobs that are indirectly connected to the industry, the total rises to almost 100,000. [16]

There are lessons to be learned from this story. 300 years of success led the Swiss watchmaking industry into a state of complacency. They had the golden goose that would lay those eggs forever. But competition emerged with the quartz movement, margins were driven down, and the Swiss watch was facing extinction. They were asleep at the wheel and suffered the demise of all companies that rest on their laurels and that prize existing products over innovative new products. They came around very late in the game and were lucky that there was still room for a trendy, well-marketed entry into a mostly saturated market.

Wang Laboratories

I started my career working as an engineer in a large company in New Jersey. My desk was among others in a sea of engineers in a room the size of a football field. This was the 60s, when calculations were performed either with the slide rule or the mechanical calculator. Two companies dominated the mechanical calculator market: Monroe and Friedan. To perform a calculation on one of these, numbers would be punched in and a hand crank would start the process. The machine would begin to grind out the answer with a series of *kerchunk-kerchunks*, as one numeral at a time appeared in the row of little windows.

One morning my boss called me into his office to demonstrate the Wang electronic calculator on his desk. This was 1965 and I had never even heard of electronic calculators. I watched as he entered two very long numbers to multiply. To my astonishment, as soon as his fingers pushed the "equals" button, the answer appeared in the window. The speed was stunning. No *kerchunks*—no waiting. He explained the purchase of these machines could be justified for his department by the savings of engineers sitting idly while their Monroes were working out their answers.

I had once visited the Monroe factory in New Jersey where their products were manufactured. It was a massive multi-story structure filled mostly with ancient metal stamping machines punching out and forming the hundreds of pieces that needed to be assembled by hand. Obviously, the electronic calculator pushed the mechanical calculator to the end of its S-Curve and eliminated an archaic, inefficient method of manufacturing office-desk equipment in factories that were dark, dirty, and dangerous.

Typical hand-assembly work station

Monroe hand-cranked mechanical calculator

Wang Laboratories, headquartered in Lowell, Massachusetts, was founded in 1951 by Dr. An Wang and Dr. G. Y. Chu. At its peak in the 1980s, Wang Laboratories—a Fortune 500 company—had annual revenues of $3 billion and employed over 33,000 people. In 1978, it was the fifth fastest growing company in America and was showing no signs of slowing down. Their corporate world headquarters building, called Wang Towers, housed 4500 employees and consisted of three interconnected 12-story structures situated on 15 acres.

Dr. Wang considered his company to be a rival of IBM,

even though Wang's market share was only a fraction of IBM's. Dr. Wang would proudly display a chart on which he had plotted Wang's growth and projected that Wang Laboratories would overtake IBM sometime in the middle of the 1990s. He hated IBM. Wang ran ads for his products on TV. He even had an ad during the Super Bowl in 1978. One showed a befuddled IBM executive working aimlessly at his desk, unaware that the view about to fill the window behind him was a Wang attack helicopter gunship taking aim at the office.

Wang Laboratories filed for bankruptcy protection in August 1992. Their Wang Towers world headquarters, built at a cost of $60 million (about $150 million in today's dollars), was sold at auction in 1994 for $525,000 and renamed Cross Point.

What happened?

This is another one of those rags-to riches-to-rags tragedies. An Wang arrived in the U.S. penniless from China in 1945. By 1951, he had earned a Ph.D. in applied physics from Harvard and patented his invention—the magnetic pulse memory core—a key component in the early PC. He started his company with $600 and began manufacturing digital electronic calculators that revolutionized the desk calculator business. He eliminated the mechanical calculator.

After successfully eliminating the mechanical calculator, Wang set his sights on eliminating the typewriter. He invented a labor-saving device — "the word processor" — a minicomputer that allowed text to be edited on a monitor screen. No longer did pages have to be completely re-typed to fix errors. Work could be stored and retrieved from memory when needed again. Multiple copies could be printed. No more carbon paper. The Wang minicomputer word processing business soared and grew over 60% a year.

Remember what happened at Kodak? Kodak's film products had reached the end of their S-Curve and executives knew that the next product to jump on was the digital camera, for which they held the patent. But they had doubts about the practicality and acceptance of digital photography and believed it would take a long time for the product to become popular.

Same with Wang; Dr. Wang would not accept the fact that the word processor was at the end of the S-Curve and about to be replaced with the PC. He was blinded by a long-held grudge against IBM, which he thought had cheated him in 1955 over the rights to his magnetic-core patents. His ego would not allow him to follow the path other PC makers were taking. Rival PC makers were all developing products to be IBM compatible, while Wang pressed on with equipment requiring a Wang operating system. That was the fatal blunder. The enormous library of software available for the IBM PC could not be directly run on the Wang PC and there were only a few available Wang-compatible software programs.

The Mouse

Xerox

Think of computer companies and you'll probably come up with names like IBM and Apple. Not Xerox.

Just as Kodak chose to ignore the opportunity it had with its patent for digital photography, Xerox ignored its chance to dominate the PC industry.

It is generally accepted that Xerox invented what we now call the PC – the personal computer. Xerox became highly successful in 1959 with their introduction of the world's first plain paper copier. They used part of the profits they earned throughout the 1960's to establish the Palo Alto Research Center (PARC) whose goal was to create the foundation for the design of all future electronic office products. In 1973, they introduced the Xerox Alto computer – one of the first computers designed specifically for personal use.

The Alto had elements we take for granted today. It had a full-page graphics monitor, a keyboard, a powerful processor, and a hard drive with removable data storage.

But two of the Alto's innovations were truly revolutionary; the ability to send typed messages to other computers in a network and the graphical user interface. Prior to the graphical interface, the user needed to type-in complex commands on the keyboard to accomplish any task. The use of what became the mouse presented the user with windows and icons with pull-down menus. For the first time, the user could create or alter documents containing text and graphics, store them and then transmit them. The Alto really never had a chance in the market as a personal computer – it had a retail price of $16,000. It did, however, inspire Steve Jobs.

In "The Creation Myth," a 2011 article in *The New Yorker*, Malcom Gladwell describes how Steve Jobs profited from Xerox's research. In 1979, twenty-four-year-old Steve Jobs, with a startup company in Cupertino, California, visited the PARC facility in nearby Palo Alto. Jobs had a demonstration of the Xerox computer there where he saw how the cursor was controlled by a "mouse." In those days, moving the cursor required typing commands on the keyboard. The button on the mouse opened and closed what were termed "windows" and moved from one task to another. He saw documents prepared on excellent word processing programs and emails exchanged with other people at PARC. Jobs went to Xerox PARC on a Wednesday or a Thursday, and on Friday met with Dean Hovey, who was one of the founders of the industrial-design firm that would become known as IDEO. He asked Harvey to develop a mouse for Apple. The Xerox mouse cost $300 to build and would break in two weeks. Jobs' instruction to the designer: "Here's your design spec: Our mouse needs to be manufacturable for less than fifteen bucks. It needs to not fail for a couple of years, and I want to be able to use it on Formica and my blue jeans."

From that meeting, Harvey says, "I went to Walgreens, which is still there, at the corner of Grant and El Camino in Mountain View, and I wandered around and bought all the underarm deodorants that I could find, because they had that ball in them. I bought a butter dish. That was the beginnings of the mouse."

Xerox began selling a version of the Alto computer in 1981. In addition to the hefty price, it was slow and underpowered, and Xerox ultimately withdrew from personal computers altogether—a catastrophic blunder.

That visit to PARC gave Jobs his inspiration. He returned from the demonstration and told his team he wanted menus on the screen, windows and a mouse. The result was the Macintosh. Years later, Jobs said, "If Xerox had known what it had and had taken advantage of its real opportunities it could have been as big as IBM plus Microsoft plus Xerox combined — and the largest high-technology company in the world." [17]

Porsche

This is a story about how a trusted Japanese advisor saved the Porsche Corporation from bankruptcy.

"If you always do what you've always done, you will always get what you've always got." The wisdom in this quote, which is often attributed to Henry Ford or Mark Twain, is what saved Porsche from bankruptcy.

In 1996, I purchased the book *Lean Thinking: Banish*

Waste and Create Wealth in Your Corporation by James P. Womack and Daniel T. Jones. While reading, I was astonished to learn that Porsche hired instructors from the Kaizen Institute in Tokyo to come to Stuttgart to help overturn their crises and change almost every aspect of Porsche; I had attended the same Kaizen Institute in Tokyo just a few years earlier. Many Japanese consultants were used at Porsche, but the principal ones were Masaaki Imai, the founder of the Kaizen Institute and the host of the study tour I attended, and Yoshiki Iwata, who led the Kaizen event at the Isuzu Trooper factory I participated in.

This chapter will describe how Porsche's CEO understood that he could no longer rely on his in-house resources to save the company. My experience with the Porsche story begins with my attendance at the Kaizen Institute, where I learned and applied the principles of lean manufacturing. Four years later, another book would give me a glimpse into the dire state of American and European auto manufacturing, including that of Porsche, which sat on the verge of bankruptcy.

THE KAIZEN INSTITUTE

In 1992, I was a senior corporate officer at Harman International Industries. Our company manufactured high-end audio equipment in factories throughout the U.S., the UK, and Europe. Foreign competition from low-wage factories in Mexico, Central America, Asia, and Eastern Europe was presenting a major challenge.

I was intrigued about the "lean" Japanese methods described in the book *The Machine That Changed the World* by Womack and Jones. A management method resulting in dramatically higher productivity, lower waste, and less inventory would certainly benefit my company. As luck would have it, Masaaki Imai—a Japanese organizational theorist and management consultant—had started the Kaizen Institute in Tokyo, offering two-week "study tours" that explained the lean management system and conducted tours of world-class factories in Japan that had successfully installed these systems. I signed up and set off for two weeks in Japan.

Our classes were held in a meeting room of Tokyo's Miyako Hotel. There were fifty-seven participants in the class I attended. I was one of two Americans; the rest were from Germany, the UK, and Asia. Twenty-nine of the participants were from Porsche, Audi, and Volkswagen—three brands from the same corporation. It was well-known at the time that Porsche was near bankruptcy. The Porsche people told me they came to Japan to learn "their secrets."

The first week of the conference consisted of morning lectures on the Toyota production system and lean principles. The lectures were all delivered in Japanese by experts in a particular aspect of lean. We wore wireless headphones to listen to the instantaneous translations. There were two translators at the back of the room who needed to switch places every twenty minutes due to the stress of the task.

Each afternoon, we boarded buses to tour factories where the specific lean process improvements described in the morning lectures had been incorporated.

The five factories were all winners of the Deming Prize, the oldest and most widely recognized quality award in the world designed to recognize companies for major advances in quality improvement. These factories were full of surprises and unlike any I had seen in the U.S., the UK, or Europe. I had expected to see examples of the latest machines, high-speed automation, and lots of robots; it was nothing like that. Most of the equipment was quite old—in some cases, over thirty years old. It was clear these factories were able to get the most out of their machines and their people.

The facility was spotlessly clean, and there was an obvious attention to "a place for everything and everything in its place." While most American factories look more like warehouses with their stacks and shelves of raw materials, work in process, and finished work, there was hardly any inventory in these "lean" Japanese factories.

The most fascinating aspect was the way they placed their machinery. In Western factories, there is typically a wide space between machines. Sometimes, this is done to allow room for storage of the material to be processed by the machines and for the output to be delivered to the next station. When an impressive, expensive machine is installed in the U.S., it is often isolated, with wide aisles created around it to allow people on factory tours to be impressed. The machines in the Japanese factories had zero space between them. Machines were pressed against each other. There was no work in process between machines, which eliminated the labor and space required to transport parts between machines. The necessity for saving space improved productivity and reduced inventory, but it was also a result of the incredibly high cost of Japanese land. Japan is a hilly, mountainous country. Most of the land is on a slope such that only 30 percent of the land is flat enough for the construction of buildings. As of 2017, land in Tokyo costs $7,600 per square foot.

None of the factories we visited relied on sophisticated computer systems to control production and inventory levels like Western companies do. They all had very simple systems using handwritten cards. Data-processing equipment was not used. This simple system called KANBAN enabled them to run their factories with 90 percent less inventory than Western factories.

Unlike most Western factories, these Japanese factories conspicuously posted their metrics so that all employees had a view of the facility's performance that hour. These metrics included pieces produced, adherence to schedule, defect rate, and more. Many Western factories either post no metrics for their employees to examine or post them to show the previous week's performance—too late, of course, to do anything about it. The productivity numbers in the Japanese factories were impressive, and the quality numbers were amazing. One of the metric boards showed one defect per million pieces produced. A Western factory would be happy with one thousand defects per million.

Prior to the trip, I thought the Japanese achieved high-quality levels by the use of Statistical Quality Control (SPC). But I saw no statistical process control charts on their metrics boards. Nobody was doing statistical charting. They were quick to point out that their quality level was not achieved by SPC, but by operator involvement in improvement efforts. The employees in each factory area were organized into teams tasked with quality and productivity improvement goals. The break rooms in each area had bulletin boards showing the status of their latest improvement activities.

All the factory workers I saw were young. It was conspicuous that they were all standing—no operators had seats. I was told they like to have young people, usually under twenty-seven years of age, working in the factories because "they are strong and can be depended upon for fresh ideas." The obvious question I had to ask was, "What happens to them after they're twenty-seven?" All but one factory said they transfer those over twenty-seven to their suppliers, who typically pay them less money. One factory manager told me those over twenty-seven years of age are trained as sales people. I didn't believe him. Until that moment, everything I observed in these Japanese factories was impressive, most particularly the degree to which management had engaged the hourly workforce. It revealed a major difference in our cultures. It's a bit like our astonishment at the very idea of Kamikaze pilots during the war.

The second week was devoted to one thing—*kaizen*. Kaizen is a Japanese word meaning "continuous improvement." This was my main reason for attending. The Japanese had spent decades developing the Toyota Production System, which was vastly more effective than mass production and made the Toyota automobile factories the most productive factories in the world. As Toyota grew, they became increasingly more dependent on suppliers. The challenge was to introduce the Toyota Production System and the associated lean management tools into these suppliers as quickly as possible.

Kaizen consultants working for Toyota were able to

transform a supplier's facility in less than five days—an astonishing achievement. This Kaizen method had been a closely guarded secret at Toyota for years, but around 1990, two senior Toyota executives who were Kaizen experts retired from Toyota and joined the Kaizen Institute to reveal their methods.

Our class was taken to the Isuzu factory, where their Trooper model was manufactured. The general manager of the facility had assembled two hundred technical employees who had been divided into teams to conduct a Kaizen "event." Our class members were distributed among the teams.

The general manager gave a speech saying that demand for the Trooper model had soared, and he tasked those of us assembled to increase output by 25 percent within the next three days. This had to be accomplished, he explained, without adding more employees, without adding overtime, and without spending money—a seemingly impossible challenge. I was assigned to a group of twelve people directed to the department that fabricated and assembled the drive shaft assembly. These twelve people had experienced many of these Kaizen events and seemed undaunted by the challenge. Our team applied the principles we had learned the week before in the Kaizen Institute classroom sessions. After the second day, our team gave our process modification ideas to that evening's night crew, who fabricated new tooling and installed them in the drive shaft area to be ready to go the next day. At the end of three days, the output of the drive shaft assembly increased by 27 percent. Our Kaizen Institute classmates reported that the Japanese Isuzu teams they were assigned to readily accepted our ideas (through interpreters). On the fourth day, all the teams presented their results to the general manager, who gave them well-deserved praise. His challenge was met and surpassed. Isuzu Trooper output increased by 25 percent with no increase in crew size, overtime, or money spent on additional machinery.

It was clear that Kaizen events were a normal occurrence at this facility and had become an accepted way of life. Lean factories in Japan typically conduct one of these Kaizen events per month. I was surprised there were no engineers on the team I was assigned to, but only management personnel participate. These non-engineers had an excellent understanding of their manufacturing processes.

Japanese design engineers in manufacturing companies are prepared very differently than their Western counterparts. Once hired, Japanese design engineers must spend their first three months in the factory working in fabrication or on the assembly line. The intent is to show them how much a difficult assembly could be improved by a better design.

I was eager to introduce the Toyota Production System, lean management, and Kaizen events at my company's worldwide facilities. We began the implementation of the Toyota Productions System at our largest facility—the 450,000-square-foot factory in Los Angeles, California where JBL loudspeakers were produced.

The improvements there were dramatic and almost immediate. Soon afterwards, the other factories in the corporation learned what happened at JBL and became eager to give it a try.

That worldwide activity occupied the next six years of my career, producing dramatically successful results. Improved productivity and quality and reduced inventory levels, delivery times, and floor space were all achieved at levels that had been previously unimaginable. Middle management was initially skeptical and resistant to these Japanese methods, but fortunately our CEO recognized we either had to change our ways or we simply would no longer be able to compete in a global marketplace. Harman International thrives to this day.

When I left Japan, I wondered whether my German classmates from Porsche would try the same techniques to help rescue their company.

The Machine That Changed The World

The same team behind *Lean Thinking* published another fascinating book on the subject called *The Machine That Changed the World*. In the book, Womack and Jones joined up with Daniel Roos to compare Japanese, American, and European automobile manufacturing. The book was the result of a five-year study they conducted for MIT's International Motor Vehicle Program (IMVP) where they were managers.

They discovered that Japanese plants (specifically Toyota), as compared to American and European plants, required:

½ the human effort

½ the space

½ the investment in tooling and automation

½ the engineering hours to develop new models

½ the new model development time

Despite conventional thinking at the time, the Japanese automaker's advantage was not the result of cheap labor, state-of-the-art, highly automated factories, currency manipulation, or government support. Their secret was a system developed by Toyota called the Toyota Production System, also known as lean production.

The American factories had changed very little since Henry Ford's introduction of what he called "mass production." The five-year study compared and contrasted lean to mass production. The lean system didn't just apply to vehicle assembly; it was used in product development and supply chain development and control.

New York Times Magazine reported, "the fundamentals of this system are applicable to every industry across the globe ... (and) will have a profound effect on human society—it will truly change the world." [18]

The study investigators discovered Toyota assembly plants have almost no rework areas, and no employees perform rework. American and European plants devoted 20 to 25 percent of their labor to fixing mistakes made by the assembly people. Toyota had the lowest number of defects per car than the best American and European plants.

General Motors Framingham Assembly Plant Versus Toyota Takaoka Assembly Plant, 1986

	GM	Toyota
Assembly hours per car	40.7	18.0
Assembly defects per car	31	16
Assembly space per car (sq. meters)	130	45
Inventory of parts (hours)	8.1	4.8

Source: IMVP World Assembly Plant survey

The comparisons show the Toyota plant to be twice as productive and twice as accurate as the American plant. In addition, Takaoka is able to change over from one type of vehicle to the next generation in a few days while changeover could take months in an American plant.

Summary of Assembly Plant Characteristics, Volume Producers, 1989
(Averages for Plants in Each Region)

	Japanese in Japan	Japanese in North America	American in North America	All Europe
Performance:				
Productivity (hours/veh.)	16.8	21.2	25.1	36.2
Quality (assembly defects/100 vehicles)	60.0	65.0	82.3	97
Layout:				
Space (sq.ft./vehicle/year)	5.7	9.1	7.8	7.8
Size of Repair Area (as % of assembly space)	4.1	4.9	12.9	14.4
Inventories (days for 8 sample parts)	0.2	1.6	2.9	2.0
Work Force:				
% of Work Force in Teams	69.3	71.3	17.3	0.6
Job Rotation (0 = none, 4 = frequent)	3.0	2.7	0.9	1.9
Suggestions/Employee	61.6	1.4	0.4	0.4
Number of Job Classes	11.9	8.7	67.1	14.8
Training of New Production Workers (hours)	380.3	370	46.4	173.3
Absenteeism	5.0	4.8	11.7	12.1
Automation:				
Welding (% of direct steps)	86.2	85.0	76.2	76.6
Painting (% of direct steps)	54.6	40.7	33.6	38.2
Assembly (% of direct steps)	1.7	1.1	1.2	3.1

Source: IMVP World Assembly Plant Survey, 1989 and J.D. Power Initial Quality Survey, 1989

Is it no wonder that American and European automobile assembly plants were unable to compete with Toyota? Note that Toyota plants had only one tenth the inventory and needed 25 percent less space—two major economic advantages.

Simply stated, Porsche, which was on the verge of bankruptcy at the time, was probably saved because their new CEO read the book *The Machine that Changed the World*, and decided to embrace lean production concepts.

THE RESCUE OF PORSCHE

In 1991, it looked like the Porsche AG company of Stuttgart, Germany, was about to go out of business.

Wendelin Wiedeking (Porsche's new CEO) recognized that his existing technical staff were unable to develop a turnaround plan for the nearly dead company. He needed trusted advisors with the experience to develop and then help implement a plan.

The Porsche company had seen its share of ups and downs over the years. It was founded by Ferdinand Porsche in 1930 as a small engineering company offering design consulting services to automobile manufacturers. He did not build any cars under his own name. One of his first clients was the German government, who gave him the assignment to design "the people's car"—quite literally, Volkswagen. This became the Volkswagen Beetle, one of the most successful automobile designs of all time.

During the war, Volkswagen production was converted to a military version of the Beetle called the "Kubelwagon" that was used similar to how the Allies used Jeeps. Porsche also designed heavy tanks like the famous Tiger for the German Army. At the end of the war in 1945, Ferdinand Porsche was arrested for war crimes and was imprisoned until 1947.

The Volkswagen factory was taken over by the British. Ivan Hirst, a British Army major, was put in charge of the factory. Volkswagen management dubbed him "the British major who saved Volkswagen."

During Ferdinand's twenty-month imprisonment, his son Perry took over the company and began his plans to manufacture a car with the Porsche name. He produced the first copy of the Porsche Model 356 by hand in 1948. A total of fifty were produced, all by craftsmen using hand tools.

Porsche Model 356

A basic Volkswagen engine was modified for the 356 and assembled into a car body mounted on a Volkswagen Beetle chassis. The Model 356 was essentially a Volkswagen with a different body and improved suspension. In 1960, the Model 356 was replaced by a completely new car, the Model 911—Porsche's most well-known and iconic model.

The Porsche company continued to grow, and by 1980 had become remarkably profitable, with sales totaling $2 billion. The Porsche company's greatest strength was its management's product engineering backgrounds and single-minded focus on the superior performance of the product itself. Unfortunately, their greatest strength was also their greatest weakness. Porsche executives developed automobiles capable of world-class performance, but they were not experienced in creating a world-class, efficient factory with dependable supply chains. Japanese automobile firms were run by executives who were familiar with not only product development, but also most of the functional areas in their companies.

Porsche's organizational structure led to inefficiency and protracted delays. The company was organized into "silos." Work proceeded by passing work from one isolated department to the next, resulting in batches of unattended work filtering through layers of management. This was exacerbated by the 1969 decision to move the product engineers to an isolated facility fourteen miles away from the factory producing their parts.

Porsche's supply base was a problem as well. They relied on 950 suppliers—a remarkably large number for a company Porsche's size. The focus was to obtain parts for superior performing cars. Unfortunately, the focus was not on cost, on-time delivery, or quality. In the 1980s, 20 percent of all parts were delivered late. Thirty percent of deliveries had the wrong number of parts, which meant that all incoming parts required inspection and, in many cases, rework. Porsche had one hundred inspectors doing nothing but sorting the good incoming parts from the bad. As a result, Porsche kept a large inventory of parts, "just in case." Unlike Toyota, Porsche did not have the capability to help their suppliers improve. This situation was the result of longtime relationships between Porsche's purchasing departments and their reluctance to leave their favorite suppliers.

One of the reasons for inefficiencies at the Porsche factory was the long cycle times. Cycle time is the amount of time a worker spends on the specific single task he is responsible for. Henry Ford, with his "assembly line," was famous for introducing and capitalizing on the short cycle time—the basis of mass production. The workers in the first Ford plant had no choice but to maintain a very short cycle time to perform their assigned tasks because they were paced by a conveyor belt that only held their work in front of them for a short time. Short cycle times allow for very brief training periods and the ability of the firm to hire inexperienced workers at low pay levels. Mass production methods had been adapted by Mercedes and the other German automobile firms. Meanwhile, Porsche relied on highly experienced craftsmen to build their cars, and their cycle times were as long as fifteen minutes. In the early years, one worker could have the pleasure to build the whole engine himself and sign it. While the worker would have a great experience and take pride in building a Porsche himself, it required many more man hours than a car built on an assembly line at a controlled pace.

The Porsche operation was a chain of inefficiency and waste. The engineers designed high-performance automobiles, but unfortunately, the designs were not manufacturable. Manufacturing engineers had to secretly redesign the parts so they could be used in the factory. The parts delivered to the factory typically did not fit together, requiring the assemblers to file and modify the part to fit (and extend the cycle time). After the car was fully assembled, a team of trouble-shooters was required to test the cars and correct the errors produced in the factory, which meant more filing and fitting. This "customization" of each car led to the need for highly-trained and experienced Porsche mechanics around the world to maintain all these nonstandard cars. Porsche had never produced a defect-free car, but after all the troubleshooting and repair at the end of the assembly line, the customer was delivered a defect-free car.

The Porsche company came crashing down in 1987 when sales began to slide as the U.S. dollar weakened against the German Mark. Porsche sold 50,000 cars in 1986, with 31,000 of those in North America. By 1992, their worldwide sales dropped to 14,000 cars and only 4,000 in North America.

Porsche needed to reorganize and cut production costs by 30 percent in order to survive, but there was no one in the company who could do it.

Wendelin Wiedeking was hired as CEO as profits dropped from $10 million in 1990 to a loss of $40 million in 1991. Porsches simply cost too much. Wiedeking read the recently released book, *The Machine That Changed the World: The Story of Lean Production—How Japan's Secret Weapon in the Global Auto Wars Will Revolutionize Western Industry*. He ordered his staff to carefully read the book and arranged for them to attend the Kaizen Institute's study tour in Japan. This could have been the very same class I attended. He not only sent the executive staff to the Kaizen Institute, he sent shop-floor workers and union members as well.

Wiedeking wanted his management team to see, firsthand, how much more efficient the Japanese automobile factories were. He took them on tours of Japanese plants to observe processes such as assembly of engines, construction of body parts and installation of dashboards and carpeting. Porsche was taking twice as long.

Wiedeking hired Japanese consultants to come to the Porsche factory. The arrival of the consultants in late 1992 was tortuous. The consultants were always polite to the workers, but often sharp with the managers. As they toured the various areas, they would stop to criticize, scold, and lecture the area managers. They would tell these experienced, highly respected German craftsmen that they didn't know what they were doing. To be spoken to in this way, in Japanese through an interpreter, in a loud voice in front of the workforce, was outrageous. These Japanese consultants came to be sarcastically labeled "insultants."

The consultants first weeklong Kaizen improvement project addressed the issue of excess inventory – a major source of wasted space, effort and money. The consultants remarked that the place looked more like a dark, disorganized warehouse than a factory.

Twenty-eight days of parts were stored in huge bins on either side of the aisle on eight-foot high shelves. An enormous amount of time was wasted by workers climbing ladders just to get parts. The height of these shelves needed to be cut in half. Nakao handed a circular saw to Wiedeking and told him to go down the aisle and cut every shelf down to four feet. No one at Porsche had ever seen something so dramatic happen so quickly without weeks of planning. At the end of just one week, the initial inventory reduction action was complete. There was no room to store twenty-eight days of parts bins. There was only room for seven days, and eventually, the parts bins were completely eliminated and there was only enough room for twenty minutes of parts. This not only reduced inventory, but radically reduced space requirements.

The consultants organized the Porsche workers into teams to improve the painting areas, the body welding shop, the engine machining shop, chassis assembly, and final assembly. The consultants would visit Porsche monthly to manage these improvement teams. The efforts resulted in a significant reduction in labor hours required to build a Porsche and, as a result, 2,500 employees were eliminated over a three-year period beginning in 1992.

Another assault was on Porsche's supply base, which was reduced from 950 to 300 firms. Much of this was the result of standardizing common parts. With the supply base reduced, Porsche engineers were able to visit these suppliers and conduct the same kind of Kaizen improvement exercises the consultants had completed at the Porsche facility.

The consultants were not only experts in manufacturing, they were experts in product development. They helped organize a team to develop Porsche's newest model, the Boxster. The car was developed in three years. Prior to that, it always took Porsche over five years to develop a new model. The Boxster was the first car ever produced by Porsche that had zero defects after final assembly.

The Porsche story illustrates the importance of leaders recognizing their inadequacies. The Porsche family realized they could no longer rely on family members to lead the company. Their decision to hire Weideking probably saved them, and Weideking's realization that he lacked the skills to turn around the mess he inherited led him to the decision to engage the Japanese consultants. It is interesting that Wendelin Weideking, who is credited for saving Porsche from the verge of bankruptcy and making it the most profitable car company in the world, was fired in 2009 for leading Porsche in an unsuccessful attempted takeover of Volkswagen. He was given a $50 million severance and went on to create the Vialino chain of pizza restaurants in Germany, Austria, and Switzerland.

This is one of those rags-to-riches-to-rags-to-riches stories. Wendelin Weideking deserves the credit for saving Porsche by embracing lean manufacturing. Today, Porsche makes over $20,000 in profit per automobile sold.

	Manu-facturing Area	Distance Car Travelled on Assembly Line	Manu-facturing Flaws	Manu-facturing Time	Managers
Before	765 Sq. Yards	455 Yards	6 per car	120 Hours	328
After	514 Sq. Yards	119 Yards	3 per car	72 Hours	226
Change	-32.8%	-73,8%	-50%	-40%	-32.2

Source – The New York Times, January 20,1996. Nathaniel C. Nash

The Final Score

EVERY KING NEEDS A JESTER

CEO's are under enormous pressures. They typically work grueling hours; are faced with rapidly changing markets, workforce, and technology; and operate in an era of ever-increasing financial and legal scrutiny.

This individual is unique in that:

• The CEO needs to hear the truth more critically than anyone else, but often he/she hears it less, or less completely, than anyone else.

• The CEO is the final decision maker.

- The CEO will be a hero when things go right, and the singular focus of attention when things go wrong.

"These realities take a toll. According to a study in the *Harvard Business Review*, two out of five new CEO's fail in the first eighteen months on the job. The major reason for their failure is not incompetence or ignorance or inexperience. Typically, CEO's are brought down because of personal behaviors influenced by hubris and ego: a need to be right, a need for admiration and adoration, a need to feel like the smartest person in the room. A study published in *Organizational Behavior and Human Decision* concluded that most powerful and successful leaders have high confidence levels. The research also indicated that the higher the self-confidence, the less likely a leader will be open to advice and feedback."[19]

The CEO of modern times is a lot like the medieval king of old. Like the king, he is most likely surrounded by a fair number of sycophants or at least people too scared to tell him the truth, scared to tell the emperor he has no clothes. And like the king, the CEO needs a jester.

Speaking Truth to Power

A jester, also called a court jester or fool, was a professional entertainer to the king and his court, and considered a member of the royal household. He was depicted on paintings of that era wearing tights with each leg a different bright color. Like the jester shown on the joker in a deck of cards, he often wore a hat and shoes tipped with bells and carried a scepter with an animal head. These men were court novelties, and negroes or dwarfs often became jesters. Paul Gallico writes of Catherine of Avila: "a large woman, who hid her dwarf jester under her voluminous skirts, and thought it great sport when he suddenly appeared with an amusing observation." A version of the jester in Britain evolved into the Punch and Judy puppet show.

In medieval times, they were skilled at singing, playing musical instruments, storytelling, juggling, and magic. But a jester was also granted "freedom of speech." Although treated as a pet, with a position of privilege within the royal household, his purpose was not only to perform, but to criticize—wittily—the master and his guests.

The comic relief at formal proceedings, he had to be ready with a joke or a barb, sometimes at the man in charge. He could voice local gossip or express unpopular sentiments without fear of royal displeasure. A clever jester directed most of his barbs at the sycophants surrounding the king. About a court lady seeking royal favor, a jester might describe her as "a beautiful wisteria, fragrant, lovely and a voracious climber." An aging pedophile reflecting on the woes of getting old heard the jester's remarks: "Lord Acton moans his lost youth, but we all know he will soon find another."

The jester was also able to blunt the edge of bad news: a battlefield loss, a new rebellion. When the French fleet was destroyed by the English in 1340 at the Battle of Sluys, King Phillippe IV's jester told him, "The English sailors don't even have the guts to jump into the water like our brave French."

Over time, the clown person morphed into someone a king or ruler trusted to speak honestly. The role was now a sounding board for opinion of the worthiness of a person or a plan. The traditional bells and costume were not used for this new intimate, who may in fact be given a title—"respected advisor."

Jester's lives and their influences on kings are important enough to have been recorded in the history books. Henry VIII of England had a jester named Will Somers. The king had a special affection for Somers, who stayed with him until the end of his life. In Henry's later years, when the pain from leg ulcers was excruciating, Will Somers was known as the only person who could make the king smile. Somers was also able to get away with joking about Cardinal Wolsey—a favorite of the king—without being executed.

Shakespeare, of course, included jesters in many of his best-known plays, using them to challenge those in authority, to reveal the reality of a situation, to say those things other characters wouldn't dare.

It doesn't take too great a leap of imagination to see a parallel in the modern world of big business. The king especially valued his jester for speaking the truth. So does the CEO today need someone with whom it's possible to have such a critical relationship. This individual is a confidante, a kind of mentor, someone who can talk openly to the boss about business realities, tell him when he's off track, and lead him to act on the best steps forward.

The following two case histories show how two very different companies were saved from going off the rails through the efforts of confident truth-tellers.

Harman International

Just as George Eastman began what we now know as the photographic industry, Sidney Harman created the high-fidelity audio industry through his international powerhouse, Harman International. But unlike Eastman, whose cognitive dissonance prevented him from changing the direction of his company, and unlike Solomon at Tower Records who denied the onslaught from streamed music, and unlike the Schwinn family who ignored the mountain bike craze, Sidney Harman did listen to trusted advisors and did adjust his company's course. That ability made the difference between Harman International going bust or enjoying, as it does today, over $6 billion in annual sales.

In the early 1950s, Dr. Sidney Harman recognized that the high fidelity (hi-fi) phenomenon, just then emerging, had the potential for rapid growth into a broad-based market. Hi-fi, began at the end of World Two and really took off at the end of the Korean War. Many veterans had technical training in the service and used the GI Bill after the war to learn electronics. The vets used these newly acquired skills to begin assembling their own music audio systems and that was the start of the hi-fi hobby and the start of the hi-fi industry.

By 1954, Harman's company had simplified high-fidelity sound for the home consumer with the introduction of the world's first true high-fidelity receiver, the Festival D1000. Before then, enthusiastic "audiophiles" needed a component called an AM-FM radio tuner to receive the radio signal and a separate amplifier to increase the signal strength sufficiently to deliver it to high performance loudspeakers. The Festival D1000 for the first time combined a tuner and power amplifier in a single chassis. Four years later, under the brand name Harman Kardon, the company brought out the world's first stereo receiver.

> **Harman Kardon invented The first true high fidelity receiver - the Festival D1000 (1954)**

Dr. Harman was on a roll. In 1969, he purchased the James B. Lansing loudspeaker company, and under his leadership the business grew rapidly. JBL loudspeakers became an exceptionally familiar brand, thanks mostly to the famous L-100, the best-selling model up to that time. The professional audio field also experienced a major expansion in the 1970s. JBL loudspeakers became popular in motion picture theaters, recording studios, sports stadiums, airports, performance venues, and the highly visible tour sound market.

> **Harman created the JBL L100 - a consumer version of their model 4300 recording studio monitor. The L100 became the largest selling loudspeaker in the industry in the 1970s. More than 125,000 pairs were sold. By 1979 recording studios in the U.S. used more JBL monitors than all other monitor brands combined.**

Harman International continued its growth plan with a string of acquisitions throughout the 1980s that more than doubled profits in the space of five years. All the while, however, the world was changing.

The International Consumer Electronics Show (CES) is a global trade show that takes place every January in Las Vegas, Nevada, in a massive complex hosting thousands of participants. There, major worldwide companies preview future products and new public announcements. Throughout the 1970s, Harman employees visiting the show or manning the company exhibits could observe that 90% of the displayed offerings were audio products—electronic boxes and loud speakers. By the early 1980s, the products were predominantly related to television. Most of the hi-fi companies who started up around the same time as Harman were gone. Brands popular in the 60's like Fisher, Scott, Sherwood, McIntosh and Marantz were no longer being sold.

Harman International was heading into oncoming traffic. Clearly, a course correction was needed.

But Sidney Harman thought he knew what he knew, and that was home audio for the consumer. After all, he had spent 29 years developing a successful corporation based on his view of the industry, and even though sales and profits were beginning to fade—as the buying public was losing interest, as competition from Asia significantly reduced profitability—Dr. Harman was determined to stay the course. Few had the courage to argue with him. Subconsciously, he probably limited his intake of new information and thinking about things in ways that didn't fit within his pre-existing convictions.

Fortunately, he was also a smart guy who, as chairman of the corporation, had worked determinedly not to surround himself with yes-men. His key staff member was his Chief Operating Officer Donald Esters. Esters recognized that the customer, the competition, and the market were shifting, and it was going to take more than a slight nudge of the steering wheel to get things back on track. He envisioned a possible solution by moving into the automobile industry.

At the time, there were no branded audio systems for automobiles. Car manufacturers installed audio components much as they installed car heaters. And Sidney Harman had no interest whatsoever in automobiles. But Esters overcame his resistance and in 1982 persuaded him to acquire a car stereo company they named Harman Motive. When he bought the small business, it was generating sales of about $8 million per year. Before the end of the decade, that division alone was reporting $100 million in annual revenues.

Under Esters leadership, Harman International convinced Ford and Chrysler to allow Harman's engineers to design customized in-dash audio systems for their cars that would incorporate eight high-quality loudspeakers and a 400-watt amplifier to create a sound as good as that in a living room. This highly profitable business expanded to include installation into cars made by GM, BMW, Mercedes, Rolls Royce and Toyota. Harman International was back on track. If not for Donald Esters, Sidney Harman's jester, the company probably would not have survived.

In the years to come, Harman International continued to reinvent itself to keep pace with changing times. The company developed the in-vehicle "infotainment" systems that enabled riders to obtain navigation information, enjoy rear-seat movies and games, send and receive text messages, make phone calls, check on traffic conditions, sports scores and weather forecasts, all via a full-color touch screen on the dashboard. Course corrections involved eliminating the physical manufacturing and shipping of bulky products by out-sourcing those operations, and concentrating instead on building large software development organizations in India and China.

In-vehicle infotainment systems manage playing audio content, navigation for driving and deliver rear-seat entertainment such as movies, games, social networking, etc., listening to incoming and sending outgoing text messages, making phone calls, and accessing Internet-enabled or Smartphone-enabled content such as traffic conditions, sports scores and weather forecasts.

These moves kept Harman International in the lucrative automotive industry. Sidney Harman's company, looking very different than it had half a century earlier, lived on. Sidney Harman assumed his success in the audio field would guarantee him success in the acquisition of Zenith Television. Fortunately, he heeded the advice of Don Esters. Unfortunately for Steve Jobs, he had no trusted advisor with his decisions on the development of Apple 2.

Sidney Harman could easily have succumbed to excess pride. He had confidence in himself because of what he had created—an empire. Sidney Harman, because of his short stature, had a bit of a Napoleonic personality which is characterized by overly-aggressive and domineering social behavior. This was typified by the extreme turnover in the executive ranks at Harman. It was the rare individual that would last more than several years in a close relationship with Harman, although surrounding himself with good people he was able to create a very substantial company. Much of that was attributable to being fortunate enough to be a part of the fad growth of the home audio industry. When that began to decline, he was again fortunate to have a small group of executives that pushed Harman into the OEM car audio business which then had phenomenal growth. Harman became famous and wealthy because of these industry developments, aided by his need for admiration, power and prestige. He did have the wisdom (dictated by his remoteness from the daily operations of the Company) to rely on the counsel of a trusted advisor.

Toyota

Take a look at the list below. How many of those names do you recognize? What do they have in common?

American Motors (1966-1987) * Apollo (1962-1964) * Aptera Motors (2005-2011) * Autoette (1948-1970) * Bricklin (1974-1976) * Checker (1922-1982) * Citicar (1974-1976) * Corbin (1999-2003) * Dale (1974) * DeLorean (1981-1982) * DeSoto (1928-1961) * Dovell (circa 1980s) * Eagle (1988-1998) * Edsel (1958-1960) * Electricar (1950-1966) * Eshelman (1953-1961) * Fiberfab (circa 1960s) * Fisker (2007-2013) * Frazen (1951-1962) * Gaslight (1960-1961) * Geo (1989-1997) * Henney (1960-1964) * Hummer (1992-2010) * Imperial (1955-1975,1981-1983) * International Harvester (1907-1975) * King Midget (1947-1970) * Mercury (1939-2010) * Nu-Klea (1959-1960) * Oldsmobile (1897-2004) * Plymouth (1928-2001) * Pontiac (1926-2010) * Powell (1930s-1960s) * Rambler (1958-1969) * Reo (1905-1975) * Saab (1937-2012) * Saturn (1985-2010) * Studebaker (1902-1969) * Stutz (1968-1987) * Vector (1971-1999, 2006-2010) * White (1902-1981) * Willys (1916-1918, 1930-1942, 1953-1963)

Who Could Forget the 2012 Fisker?

This is, in fact, a rundown of defunct car companies since 1960. The only surviving manufacturers that never declared bankruptcy are Ford and Tesla.

It's particularly interesting that a Toyota model isn't on that list in light of the catastrophic introduction of the brand to North America in 1958. That was when Toyota imported two sample Toyopet Crown sedans to the U.S. and established headquarters in a former Rambler dealership in Hollywood, California. They sold a total of 287 Toyopet Crowns that year, list price $2,300.

Toyopet Crown

It was a terrible car. The engine was severely under-powered. The vehicle had poor high-speed stability, was extremely noisy, vibrated uncontrollably, and parts broke constantly. Yet Toyota grew from that miserable entry into the market to become the number one retail brand in 2015. A large part of that rise can be attributed to a most unusual jester to the king.

A review of 20th century Japanese history helps understand the company's phenomenal success. Prior to WW II, Japan was a feudal nation with slight manufacturing capabilities. "Made in Japan" tended to signify cheap, poor quality, or an inferior copy of something from the West.

Prior to Japan's manufacturing revolution in the 1950s, "Made in Japan" meant "Junk"

After Japan's surrender in August 1945, American forces under the leadership of General Douglas MacArthur occupied the country. MacArthur effectively oversaw post-war development from 1945 to 1951, during which period he initiated sweeping political and social reforms that included women's rights, separation of church and state, a constitution based on the American constitution, and the introduction of labor unions. The Japanese came to view MacArthur as a liberator from the brutal rule of the military, from war, and from poverty. There are still statues of MacArthur in Japan.

Among the occupation forces working under General MacArthur was an obscure American statistician, William Edwards Deming. His research came to the attention of industrial leaders around 1950, including the heads of the Toyota Motor Corporation, established in 1933 by Kiichiro Toyoda. Deming was invited to give a series of lectures on manufacturing management, and he and his message were eagerly embraced.

The Japanese knew they would recover and prosper only if they could sell products on world markets, and the obstacles were immense. Seventy percent of Japan's land is severely sloped. Land available for factory construction is fabulously expensive. The country has no natural resources. Simply copying American methods wouldn't work, for America had unlimited land for expansion, unlimited raw materials, and a domestic market that could absorb all that the factories could deliver. Japan needed to develop a "poor man's" manufacturing system, one that allowed a factory to produce with limited available space, limited manpower, fewer wasted materials, fewer defects, and fewer field failures.

Deming had some answers. The CEOs listened. And what evolved for one company is known as the Toyota Productions System, the basis for the development and production of Toyota cars.

Although much of what Deming taught the Japanese was the use of statistics to improve quality, his most important idea was PDCA: PLAN-DO-CHECK-AD-JUST. Based on the scientific method developed from the work of Francis Bacon in the 17th century, it's an essentially simple concept: Observe the situation; come up with an explanation for the observation (a hypothesis); test the hypothesis for validity; then, either act on the hypothesis (as the best course of action at the moment) or reject it and try to come up with a better one.

A Toyota PLAN would determine the objectives and processes necessary to deliver results for a particular goal, which might be, for example, to increase the output of rearview mirrors in a factory using the existing number of people.

The plan would be implemented, making any designed changes to equipment, worker assignment, and so on. Performance would be constantly monitored.

Management would CHECK the results. How many mirrors were produced?

If the output matched the original plan, a new standard method for manufacturing rearview mirrors was established. If not, ADJUSTMENTS would be made and a new PDCA cycle was initiated. Multiple cycles were to be repeated until the objective was achieved.

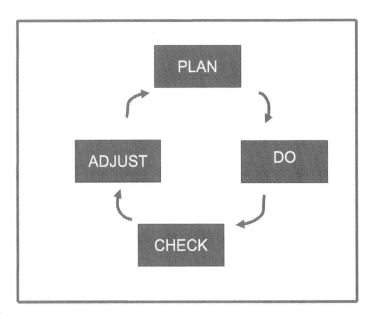

The letters PDCA stand for the four-step process; Plan, Do, Check, Adjust. The concept is typically represented by a wheel to illustrate the point that PDCA is a repeated cycle. It's the repetition of the cycle that assures continuous improvement of processes.

In Deming's view, PDCA allowed people and organizations to continually improve themselves, their relationships, their processes, products, and services. His overriding philosophy was one of cooperation and eye-on-the-goal; it avoided blame and encouraged individuals to view mistakes as opportunities to reach the next best step. PDCA was in large measure what kept Toyota's senior management paying attention to signals that they were heading into oncoming traffic. They reacted smartly and quickly to the Toyopet Crown flop.

The company established a goal for itself in the 1950s, which was stated simply: "To Become the World's Largest Automobile Producer." And it did achieve that distinction, eventually overtaking GM and Volkswagen. Success required constant adjustments over the years—for currency changes of the yen vs. the dollar, for example; for rising labor and material costs; for market shifts. The PDCA approach.

Pontiac didn't take that approach. And it disappeared. In business since 1926, Pontiac enjoyed a reputation as producer of performance cars at comfortable prices, becoming at one point the third-most-popular domestic car brand in America. But by the early 1980s, the name became emblematic of GM's plan to make all their brands share common platforms. Pontiac had lost its distinction, and the deterioration was a slow decline, a gradual drifting into oncoming traffic. Younger buyers moved over to import brands, and left Pontiac marketing to older owners in the shrinking market of domestic "muscle cars." Production ended in 2010.

Toyota learned its lessons well. Japan eventually became expert in manufacturing, and today, a "Made in Japan" label signifies high quality and innovative design. No one forgot William Edwards Deming. The Deming Grand Prize or the Deming Medal was established as the Japan Quality Medal in 1951 (the name change took place in 2012). To this day, Japanese companies and individuals strive to achieve this oldest and most widely recognized quality award in the world, which is described: "The Deming Medal is presented to those who, like Dr. Deming, have successfully combined the application of statistical thinking and management so that each supports and enhances the other, thus leading to quality in products and services."

There's another kind of individual who can be counted on to speak truth to power. This is the executive coach.

THE EXECUTIVE COACH: AN OUTSIDE AND TRUSTED SET OF EYES

Most elite athletes have coaches. So do many business leaders, who hire an informed person for the specific purpose of providing an outsider's insight and advice.

Some of our most famous CEO's swear by the practice.

Eric Schmidt, Chairman and CEO of Google: "My best advice is to have a coach. Once I realized I could trust him [his coach] and that he could help me with perspective, I decided it was a great idea."

Jonathan Schwartz, former President and CEO of Sun Microsystems, said many CEO's are reluctant to admit they had a coach. "The cost of executive coaches, particularly a good one, is not cheap, but compared to the decisions CEO's make, money is not the issue. If you have a new perspective, if you feel better with your team and the marketplace, then you received real value."

Steve Bennet, former CEO of Intuit: "At the end of the day, people who are high achievers—who want to continue to learn and grow and be effective—need coaching."

William R. Johnson, CEO of H.J. Heinz Company: "Great CEO's, like great athletes, benefit from coaches that bring a perspective that comes from years of knowing you, the company, and what you need to do as CEO to successfully drive the company forward. Every CEO can benefit from strong, assertive, basic and honest coaching."

As Jonathan Schwartz said, coaches don't come cheap. Some charge as much as $3500 an hour for their services. As William Johnson suggested, the relationship may continue over a long period, perhaps years of repeated "tune-ups" to adapt to changing needs and challenges. And as some CEO's who have benefitted from coaching will acknowledge, the process often involves coming to grips with uncomfortable personal shortcomings. A coach who's doing his job will be chipping away at any cognitive dissonance that's getting in the way of success.

> William R. Johnson, CEO of the H. J. Heinz Company said, "Great CEO's, like great athletes, benefit from coaches that bring a perspective that comes from years of knowing you, the company and what you need to do as CEO to successfully drive the company forward. Every CEO can benefit from strong, assertive, basic and honest coaching." Bill Gates, co-founder of Microsoft said, "Everyone needs a coach. It doesn't matter whether you're a basketball player, a tennis player, a gymnast or a bridge player."

There's a wonderful quote from Konosuke Matsushita (he died in 1989), the fabulously successful entrepreneur and founder of Japan's General Electric, the $65 billion Matsushita Electric Company. One of the largest exporters of electric equipment to the U.S., it includes the brand names Panasonic and JVC

Change of thought makes your behavior change.

Change of behavior makes your habits change.

Change of habit makes your personality change.

Change of personality makes your destiny change.

Matsushita's is an amazing and inspirational rags-to-riches story. Born into poverty, he began working at age four and by age nine, was in an apprenticeship demanding a sixteen-hour day. At 22, he invented a new type of electrical socket, started manufacturing it, and turned that small shop into an international industrial giant. In addition to creating an empire, Matsushita wrote dozens of management books, founded a graduate school of leadership, created Japan's version of the Nobel Prize, and gave away hundreds of millions to charity.

Konosuke Masushita, a fabulously successful enrepeneur and founder of Japan's General Electric, the $65 billion Matsushita Electirc Company, one of the larget exporters of electric equpment to the U.S. under such brand names as Panasonic and JVC.

Changing the destiny of a company might have to begin with changing how the CEO thinks.

A major failing of the CEO, as we've seen over the past chapters, is a lack of self-awareness, and the gap between how a senior executive sees himself vs. how others see him is often a root cause for resistance to change. As a leader's power increases, he is more likely to ignore or misunderstand the input he gets from those with less authority. He assumes that his subordinates' insights match his own—and no one has the courage to challenge him. By reducing the gap, this blind spot, and delivering useful feedback, the coach ideally creates a more constructive atmosphere.

Sports coaches often teach athletes to execute plays that will defeat the competition, moves the other guy doesn't anticipate. Business coaches are not about defeating the competition. Years ago, a business coach typically was brought in by the company to help save the talented but nasty senior executive who would probably have to be fired if he didn't straighten out. The CEO coach today does not serve a remedial function. He's there to help his client learn how to establish goals and eliminate barriers to enhanced high performance.

He's somewhat different from a consultant, who also takes on the role of trusted advisor. Consultants typically are technical experts hired to serve a particular problem. Their assignments are usually for a short term. The coach, on the other hand, supports the client over a period of time in achieving his own results by building on his own strengths.

Anyone can announce himself as a CEO coach. There's no special degree or accreditation required. Most coaches to well-known business leaders are not psychologists or from executive search firms. Typically, they are themselves retired CEO's from related industries, or experts from government, universities, or think tanks.

EXECUTIVE COACHES

Mike McKay

Part of the job, says Mike McKay, a partner in Action-COACH of Madison, LLC, is helping the executive "learn that people are people, not things. We believe all executives have leadership skills. We show them how to use those skills in a way that makes achieving the results they want significantly easier and actually makes work fun again."

It starts with changing how a CEO thinks.

Mike McKay is a partner in ActionCOACH of Madison, LLC. ActionCOACH provides executive level business coaching focused on one thing—profit growth. Mike can be reached at mikemckay@actioncoach.com.

Mike McKay: *"Why Don't They Just Listen?"*

According to McKay, this, or words like them, is what he often first hears from a client. The client is thinking that if everyone else would just "do their own jobs," the executive would be successful doing his or her own.

And that, says Mike McKay, is never the case.

Here, in his own words, is how a CEO coach achieves results:

We are all guilty of "expectational ESP," an unconscious belief that if we know or have experienced something, all those around us learned (or kind of) the same lesson at the same time. Somehow.

And then, there's the "I learned this by being thrown in the water and learning to swim, why can't they?" phenomenon. Well, if "they" were talented enough to do that, "they" would probably have your job and none of this would be an issue. Ultimately, this is a copout by the executive to let himself off the hook for having to develop his own team.

Executive coaching is a trust-based relationship. As a coach, when I need to push executives to break through some old habit or a behavior that is not serving them well, they won't accept the coaching if they don't trust me. This is often the only relationship where the executive can share real challenges, fears, hopes, and dreams. They can't tell their boss for fear of losing face. And they can't tell their people for fear of exposing some weakness. (Spoiler: All the people around you already know your weaknesses. They're just too nice or too frightened to tell you!)

There are three ways that I establish trust.

First, the relationship is confidential. Period. If there is something I think the company needs to know, I'll either coach the executive through how to have that conversation with the boss, or I'll ask permission to have the conversation myself. If the client says no, then it's no.

Second is our on-boarding process. During a typical on-boarding, we discuss the rules of the coaching re-lationship—showing up when you're scheduled, doing the work you commit to doing, etc. My preference is to start new clients face-to-face, so I can get the "measure" of the person. After a couple hours, I know the person well enough to know when he's bullshitting me.

And finally, "throwing the flag." You know, those little yellow things that referees throw? I know enough commonalities among executive challenges that I can usually tell when someone is trying to snow me. And if so, that is a point in the conversation where we stop and I throw the flag. I let him know that I care about his success and I'm the person who's not going to let him get away with his own bullshit anymore. Those are the critical junctures where I earn the client's trust.

Here are two stories that demonstrate the range of challenges that coaching can help you to overcome.

Susan was a Division Vice President in a major corporation. She had a cast of junior leaders working for her and her patience level was incredibly low. She said she believed in her team and that they were talented and very inexperienced. Her behavior, displayed completely different messages.

She'd grown up in the "sink or swim" training culture of her division—if it was good enough for the senior executives, it should be good enough for the employees—and had been extremely successful. Susan could be forgiven for thinking that was the right approach. But the results showed otherwise. In addition, her work hours were extremely long and stressful—stress that she took out on her team.

I coached Susan that life is a mirror. She was getting back exactly the behavior she was modeling. Worse, since she was always willing to "fix" her team's failures—usually with a comment like "if you want something done right…," they simply let her do the job by never living up to her expectations. Why would they ever give her their best work?

Susan needed to learn that people are in one of two places. Either they don't know how to do the thing they are asked to do, or they choose not to do it. But you must observe which one it is before you can manage them correctly.

Once Susan realized she was the main problem, through a few uncomfortable (for her) conversations, we started working on true accountability for her team and delegation on her part. That doesn't mean yelling and screaming at people for not doing what you think they should do. It involves learning to coach them through commitments, and giving them what they need to achieve them. And if they don't, it means actual consequences.

We set three tasks. First, the team had to improve Gross Profit Percentage. Next, they had to create a new business development plan. Finally, they would need to focus on true revenue growth from the core business.

In every case, we found an actual skill gap. Not a "those guys are lazy and just don't do their jobs" gap—a factual situation in which the team did not know how to perform their tasks. But let's face it; most executives aren't really welcoming of employees telling them "we don't know how" to do something. Prior to coaching, Susan wasn't open to that input.

Of course, once we identified skill gaps, Susan's team was responsible for actual training, and not the "throw 'em in the water" kind. As they learned what true accountability meant, the results began to improve. Gross profit growth exceeded the improvement target. Sales are finally showing sustainable growth after four months of work.

And Susan works fewer hours; in fact, everyone in the division works fewer hours.

A second example:

Executive coaching is a highly leveraged tool in preparation for promotion. Bill was the CFO of a large organization, which asked me to help determine if he was a good candidate for CEO. Once again, the culture of the business was not conducive to people doing good work. Many executives still think that micro-managing individuals is a legitimate strategy, but in this organization it was rampant.

Fortunately, Bill didn't see much value in continuing that process.

With the current CEO's support, Bill started an executive coaching program with me. I don't believe that at the time Bill considered himself a CEO candidate. However, he knew at a gut instinct level that the people in the business were not fully engaged or doing their best work. I coached Bill to start a "shadow" program.

He did this on his own—no help or input from his peers or the CEO. And what he found was eye-opening. Employees couldn't believe that Bill was talking to them about what they were really going through. It took a few weeks for them to believe he didn't have an ulterior motive.

As they saw him responding to and actually fixing some of the issues they told him about, they became more engaged. To this day, months after beginning his program, Bill visits with his employees for two to three hours one afternoon each week. I know he does this because we talk about his results at our coaching sessions.

Not only did the board of directors learn about Bill's process, he was creating financial momentum for the company. This happened at a time when their industry was going through significant upheaval leading to large losses, and Bill's team ultimately delivered the first month of profitability in four years. He had created enough credibility with the board that no other outside candidate made it to the last step of the search process. Bill was named the next CEO of the company.

When I say coaching involves some tough conversations, I mean they are tough on the clients. Most don't want to hear that they are the problem. And sometimes, they need to hear it week after week, with specific examples that demonstrate the problematic issues. The coach's role is not training or technical development. Most executives know more than enough technical stuff to succeed in their jobs. The coach's role is to hold up a mirror to help the client see what he's doing that's getting in the way. We help the executive first change how he thinks about his team. He comes to see them not as "replaceable cogs," but as individuals who want to do good work. He believes that developing them is what leads to actual success. And then we help him create new behaviors that get the results he wants. Pretty crazy that something that simple can be so dramatic.

If there is one key idea I implore every executive to understand, it's this: There really aren't many individuals in the world who want to get up in the morning and disappoint you. The vast majority of your people are trying to do their best and earn their paychecks.

Larry Broughton

Larry Broughton is an award-winning entrepreneur and CEO, bestselling author, serial entrepreneur, keynote speaker, and former Special Forces Operator. As a former U.S. Army Staff Sergeant, serving 8 years on Special Forces A-Teams (commonly known as the Green Berets), Larry has parlayed the lessons learned from his time in service to his country and applied them to the business arena, attaining extraordinary success.

He is the Founder & CEO of broughtonHOTELS (www.broughtonHOTELS.com), a leader in the boutique hotel industry; BROUGHTONadvisory (www.BROUGHTONadvisory.com), a strategic vision, elite team building, and transformational leadership training company; as well as yoogozi.com, an inspirational online learning forum for leaders and high achievers. Larry has received several business awards, including Ernst & Young's *Entrepreneur of the Year*®; the National Veteran-Owned Business Association's *Vetrepreneur® of the Year*; Coastline Foundation's *Visionary of the Year*; Passkeys Foundation's *National Leader of Integrity;* and *Entrepreneur Magazine* included his firm on their *Hot 500 List of Fastest Growing Private Companies.*

Larry has authored several articles and books on leadership, team building, and entrepreneurial significance, including *VICTORY: 7 Entrepreneurial Success Strategies for Veterans* and his most recent *FLASHPOINTS for Achievers.* His upbeat, creative approach to business and life has been featured in newspaper and magazine articles across the country and he's been a guest on news and TV programs on every major network, including multiple appearances on **CNBC's** *The Big Idea with Donny Deutsch*, **MSNBC's** *Your Business* **with JJ Ramberg, and Travel Channel's hit show,** *Hotel Impossible.*

Larry has presented to, coached, and mentored thousands of current and aspiring leaders and entrepreneurs across the country. He has delivered keynote addresses and training programs on topics including entrepreneurship, leadership, and overcoming fear and failure to Fortune 100 firms, universities, non-profits, medical facilities, and even the **Pentagon's** Office of the Chairman of the Joint Chiefs of Staff.

Larry has attended the Executive Program at prestigious Stanford University; studied Russian at the world-renowned Defense Language Institute; and Political Science at University of California, Santa Barbara and College of San Mateo.

For more information on Larry, please visit www. LarryBroughton.me

Most of my clients come as referrals from current or past clients, so they hear firsthand from folks who have worked with me about the confidential, upbeat, direct, and respectful nature of the relationships I build. These direct referrals help expedite the Know, Like, and Trust factor that every business needs to attract and retain clients. Additionally, I share with potential clients (prior to our first session) tragedy to triumph stories and lessons that have come from my own failings, missteps, and mistakes. I also share social proof, testimonials, and case studies from past clients who have overcome obstacles and challenges using the systems, processes, and mindset techniques they've learned from our programs.

In some cases, we conduct 360 Degree Reviews and

Peer Reviews, but in every case administer strengths-based assessments of key team members to identify conative strengths to assure they have the right team members in the right seats of their business, and that team members are fully engaged, which leads to higher morale, increased productivity, and soaring profits.

Several success stories come to mind. Since I sign confidentiality agreements with my clients, I'm giving you general broad stroke answers.

An aspiring entrepreneur wanted to launch a Health & Fitness Company targeting young people who had a desire to enter the military by presenting customized workout routines based on their current capabilities. He had been working on the idea for nearly two years and was unable to get the plan launched. He felt strongly that the U.S. military needed recruits to show up to basic training in better shape, which would lead to better training results and higher performing soldiers, sailors, airmen, and Marines. The problem was multi-pronged: The entrepreneur had no experience in the Health & Fitness industry, he did not know anyone in the industry, he was not personally driven by nor passionate about Health & Fitness, and was not living a healthy lifestyle (which meant it would be difficult for him to be the face of the organization).

After some strengths, skills, and resource assessments, he realized that he was not the person who could successfully launch or lead this type of endeavor. He was dejected and demoralized for a moment when he realized this really was not going to be feasible, but during the awakening process he found the courage to share his BHAG (Big Hairy Audacious Goal): to launch a mobile medical care company to serve Third World, developing and frontier nations. This idea, much bolder than his Health & Fitness idea, required more capital, stronger logistics, and bigger thinking. It did, however, tap into his current strengths, skills, and resources. He was a former logistics officer in the U.S. Army; worked for several years in the medical device industry; had deep contacts in the medical field, as well as former special operations medical personnel who would lead the mobile teams; had a love for cutting-edge technology and communications platforms (which would be vital to this business); and he was absolutely passionate about the idea. He realized this was the business he should be launching. Because of our work together, he was able to put together a Board of Advisors, raise capital, hire key team members, and launch the business in under one year.

Mike Bartlett

Mike Bartlett is the *Managing Director and Owner of Agilis Solutions Ltd; a Business Strategy (Development & Delivery) and Executive Coach Service based close to London in the UK.*

Agilis Solutions has developed repeatable methodologies that allow Businesses to really test their focus on their products and customers and to make corrections or changes to their business strategies and delivery to maximize their medium-term successes.

Mike can be reached directly at mike@bartsbase.com

Mike Bartlett: *"It's all about the people."*

How you maximize people's focused contributions, how you ensure staff and customers alike know and understand what you are about; how you ensure you interface and interact with outsiders that could influence the future success of your business (in a good or a bad way !)—this is the core of my coaching efforts.

We help executives prioritize their focus on the issues that matter most to the business at that time, and on the medium-term horizon, that impact that most important outcome, sustained profitability.

Key to our success is to build a close and trusting relationship with the executive, often the CEO of the business; to become his / her eyes and ears as well; and essentially to ensure that all changes or cultural developments come directly from the executive in their own words and style.

Here's how I reason when working as a CEO coach. The most critical challenge for a CEO is not to lose sight of the essential reasons for the success of his / her business. That there are a million things a CEO has to deal with and get involved with and many CEOs gravitate to the areas and issues that they enjoy most or get the most satisfaction from. But there are certain elements of the business that *keep* them in business and can simply *NOT* be ignored.

A common way to keep track of these is to create a "dashboard" of the few, but most important parameters of the business.

The designers of your car gave you six gauges on the dashboard for you to continually monitor your car's performance: speed, fuel level, water temperature, oil pressure warning light, battery charge, and tachometer. Just six "indicators." They could have added more gauges, like exhaust gas temperature and actual oil pressure, but those are not necessary as first line indicators of your car's immediate performance. The six on the dashboard are all that is needed.

Surprisingly, CEO's are often missing one or more of the necessary gauges on their company's "dashboard." The most obvious one is **true profitability**, which, in turn, if not managed fastidiously leads to cash issues and then the most common cause of business failure—insolvency. You would be surprised at how many companies I work with which are not in control or aware of all the elements of profitability.

Another key example is remaining directly in tune with your customer base.

If the customer is unhappy with the treatment they receive, or if the product or service is only just good enough, or if they feel you are not moving with the times (in terms of product evolution, for example), then your business is at risk. So when I coach with a CEO, it's most important I get to understand the business, not purely from talking with the CEO, but also by interacting with senior staff and customers, all of whom see the coach as an ally—someone who is not upset to hear about issues they believe (often incorrectly) the CEO is not easily receptive to. This process allows me to steer the focus and discussion with the CEO to areas that perhaps need greater involvement or change driven from the CEO.

In particular, it allows me, when this is the case, to bring to the CEO's attention the fact that there is reticence amongst the staff to speak openly. In my experience, this is a very common situation and most CEO's are unaware of it, but are keen to fix it and grateful to be made aware of it. It comes about usually from lack of time spent interacting with staff at all levels, which is interpreted as "no interest in us."

I can also point him / her in the right direction to find other expertise or current best practice. This latter is very important and essential for a Coach to be tuned-in to, and is one of the reasons a CEO will feel comfortable with a coach, kind of like an arm to hold onto. It is of course the CEO who rolls out any changes.

Here are two examples:

I worked with the CEO of a large print company producing high-profile weekly and monthly magazines—a high-volume business with prestigious publisher clients. In conversation with him initially I detected concern over the poor bottom line, some months negative, some months positive. But it was, he said, a seasonal business. The CEO had at least detected that something was going wrong but he had missed that there were fundamental operating problems driving the poor profitability results.

Somewhere in the past, short-term profit considerations had driven a previous CEO to cut expenditure on anything that he did not perceive brought immediate bottom line benefit. People development and machine maintenance were two of many activities that his axe fell upon. The medium-term consequences were dramatic. A closer look at the manufacturing facility, which looked busy, revealed that although the presses seemed full, the shop floor had to deal with so many interruptions and quality issues that the true production was probably way off where it should be. The manufacturing was left to an old hand with 30 years' service in the print industry, someone who at first glance you would expect to be on top of this process-driven operation.

The CEO, who was not a manufacturing guy, assumed the print manager was an expert after all those years in the industry.

However, this man had never modernized his management techniques and tools; in fact, it turned out that the business had never really felt it necessary to allocate time and money to developing its staff's skill base.

Further examination showed there were no measures applied to the shop floor performance and no expectations set, other than "get this out on time".

This was, on the face of it, an extraordinary situation—that such a key mechanism of the business should not have any measures around its real performance. How could the business know if it were competitive with its rival suppliers? How could it know where it stood on a world scale of performance? And how could it drive improvement? The answer is it could not do any of those things!

Two points come out of this: firstly, how important an outside and trusted set of eyes can be and second why it pays to take the time to carefully create a "dashboard" for your business—it is an essential tool to keep any business "sharp."

When the CEO introduced an OEE (overall equipment efficiency) measurement technique at my suggestion, we found that utilization was probably only half of where it should be. Imagine all these multimillion-dollar machines running at half speed, in effect; no wonder the profits were eroded. Putting it right was a whole other story. Part of the solution required cash to fix or replace parts that were worn or damaged parts that caused other parts to wear. The "check" was going to be a lot more than if the machines had been maintained regularly.

On top of that, it was necessary to develop techniques to standardize the processes involved in running the presses, because in the absence of measures and with varying degrees of failure, every crew will have developed its own "best shot" at getting the magazines produced.

One thing is certain: the customer will have noticed an unsatisfactory product. But the customer will up to a point have tolerated it, largely because it is not easy to swap suppliers and so inertia kicks in, which also gives a false sense of security to the supplier.

Another interesting issue that falls out of this is the observed reluctance of employees in many businesses to point out what they see as obvious failings in the way the business is performing.

In this case, shop floor employees knew that the lack of maintenance of their complex machinery was affecting, slowly but surely, their ability to produce consistently and predictably; but no one dared question the previous decision to reduce or stop expenditure. Everyone assumed it was a decision made for a "good reason." Whether it was from fear of reprimand for questioning a superior or a genuine belief amongst employees that they had to work within the constraints handed down to them, the net effect on the business could only be described as calamitous.

Employee involvement in running a business in a structured manner is vital to the fine-tuning of and focus on delivery. Indeed, staff morale and consultative involvement could well be a "gauge" on the "dashboard."

It is certainly one of the tools to develop an open culture in the workplace, one where in general employees feel so much happier about their role and contribution. All of which benefits, guess what, the *BOTTOM LINE.*

A second example was working with the CEO of a service company that had a huge contract to manage all the computer services, facilities management, and building works of a multi-site government organization.

Because these contracts are won on tenders to the lowest bidder, the CEO typically focuses on managing the margin, which is rarely more than a few percent. In this instance, I discovered that the CEO had little practical time for the customers because of all the detailed involvement with his human cost-base. However, talking with the customer, we discovered they were very dissatisfied with the level of service and of the attitude of the people delivering the services. I found there were no measures in place that directly assessed performance from a customer perspective, only measures around employee cost, overtime costs, material costs etc.

When we introduced measurements of on-time delivery, we found it was only 70%—no wonder the customer was unhappy.

Clearly we had indicators missing from our "dash-board": "Customer Satisfaction" as well as "On time Delivery," both obvious in hindsight but once again missed in the CEO's thinking.

Why was this? Largely because the CEO was responding solely to the continued pressure and demands placed on him by his group bosses, which were purely financial. Again, this is a common scenario in my experience.

Working with the CEO, we developed a raft of changes, both to the operating practices and to interactions with the customer. Regular discussion forums with the customer allowed the CEO to fine-tune the skill-base and manner of the delivery end of the business, as well as to really understand which services were the most critical to the customers' business operation and which were merely supportive.

This allowed a huge improvement in the perceived quality and timeliness of the services provided and a jump in understanding by all employees of the importance of what they contributed and, most importantly, where it fit into the "big picture." The CEO was heralded as a savior by his group bosses and by the customer, and this turn-around led ultimately to the offer of a further series of multi-million dollar contracts from the same customer.

The third example was with the CEO of a high-tech capital goods company, designing and manufacturing products which supported the sale of consumables from another part of the group.

Again, the CEO focused on manufacturing to cost and getting products out of the door.

A third of the employees of this company worked in R&D and R&D had the capacity to invent more and more complex products using state-of-the-art technology. R&D were a law unto themselves; no one questioned R&D!

However, although at the time the CEO didn't realize this, customers didn't like the products because they were expensive *and* unreliable, but they had to buy them to use the consumables that they *did* like.

This revelation allowed the CEO to refocus onto product design, and to introduce some modern techniques in part quantity reduction as well as ease of manufacture.

From this, together with consultative meetings with customers around the world from which he gained a new understanding of the customers' needs, in terms of features, performance and method of use, he was able to arrive at products that were reliable, actually cheaper to produce, and fulfilled all the customers' needs.

The next generation products designed with help from outside experts alongside the huge R&D department had 35% less components, had standardized parts used wherever possible, and were 60% faster to assemble!

They also had the "ease of use" features that customers wanted so badly and because of reduced complexity were found to be more reliable in use.

This was a 2-year major program, so it required support from the parent company, which the CEO, from his intimate knowledge gained through the initial exercise, was easily able to convince them of its importance and thus support.

As a consequence, sales numbers and profit shot up, sales by some 40% over 3 years and profit by a much larger number!

In these examples, the coach facilitated the CEO to refocus or rebalance his activities to the current, most critical issues, and as a result dramatically improve the performance, profitability, and safety of his organization.

You would be surprised at how many companies do not have a well-thought-through dashboard of measures, such as Customer Satisfaction, On Time Performance, Employee contribution, and even Profitability.

The role of Coach to the CEO is a great way to allow "intelligent outside eyes" into a business in a trusted manner and help the Executive reshape his business in a non-judgmental manner.

Lynn Davidson

Lynn Davidson
Executive Coach
London, England

Lynn Davidson is a sought-after executive coach in England. She described an engagement where the board decided the CEO needed a coach. This CEO was performing adequately but while one faction of the company respected and admired him, another faction feared and hated hm. She knew that prior to becoming a senior executive he had been a popular professional soccer player. According to Lynn, Professional Soccer players in the UK are treated like rock stars—especially if they are good looking like David Beckham. These people are also notorious for their arrogance and Lynn detected that arrogance instantly at their first session.

In that first session, a board member invited the CEO into a meeting to meet Lynn Davidson, who he described was being hired to coach him. At that session with the three of them in the board room, the CEO was suitably polite and spent his time bragging about himself. The Board member left the two of them alone and at that point, Lynn said, "If we're going to get along I would advise you not to fuck with me and don't try blowing smoke up my ass. I'm here to do a job that's not about you telling me what you're good at. It's to correct the issues that are causing lack of trust in you. If you insist in telling me things that make you feel good about yourself, we will never progress from this first meeting." She said that after that moment, they got along great and he was open to her advice.

She explained to me that she knew she had to deal with an alpha male who would reject another alpha male as an advisor. She knew she had to convince him she was tough, while at the same time "seemed cuddly."

CONCLUSION

Now that you have finished this book, I hope you got the message that the things that brought down all those famous CEO failures could have been avoided.

I wrote in this book's preface that 88% of the companies on the S&P 500 in 1955 are gone. The business world has a Darwinian culture where *survival of the fittest* prevails.

Edison, Kodak, Tower Records, Polaroid, and Blockbuster did not survive. Here are some questions about company failures in terms of the "Five Mistakes" outlined in this book.

Did Tower Records understand that streaming music was inevitable?

Was it made clear to Land that instant photography was losing popularity?

Did Blockbuster's Antioco recognize that Netflix had a superior product?

Why didn't executives of the Swiss watch companies know that they needed to develop new technology?

Why did Edison believe he couldn't be wrong about DC current?

Why did Kodak take so long to finally begin work on digital photography?

Why did Schwinn never get around to modernizing their Chicago factory?

These are the mistakes that prevent the CEO from reacting decisively to the reality that the company is in the midst of a crisis and heading towards failure.

Companies like LEGO, Harman International and Nissan did survive. They were open to advice from people with fresh eyes. And that is the point of this book. Leaders today, probably more than ever, need an outsider to look at the situation in a *different* way.

There is benefit to having "new eyes." In most cases, the outsider will not be prejudiced by the situation he is brought in to observe. It is often very difficult for CEO's to be able to be critical of their own plans, even when they look back at performance over the past years and see the plan isn't working. Intel's Andy Grove's sage advice, "Only the Paranoid Survive," could have saved these failed organizations.

One of the benefits of bringing in an outsider is that the act itself creates a crisis atmosphere. People's attention gets focused and a crisis atmosphere often encourages cooperation (in order to survive). It's an unusual CEO who has the courage to create a crisis atmosphere and announce, "This company is in trouble, we will not survive unless we all change."

Many CEO's won't do that because they often are having a "romance with the familiar" and a resultant fear of change. Most people would welcome certain changes in their lives. Winning the lottery would be a pleasant change because the result would be clear. But most changes in life have unknown results and are, therefore, typically feared.

The outsiders who are brought it to turn companies around are highly experienced and highly analytical. They are able to quickly formulate a get-well plan by gaining an understanding of the client's situation, typically by speaking to as many people as possible.

Ghosn's turnaround plan for Nissan was remarkable. He was quoted in an interview at Stanford Graduate

School of Business, "The best way to look for a solution is to interview as many people as possible, particularly people in critical process areas. Let me go see the people who are in charge of the process or around this process, interview them and ask, 'What's wrong? What do you think is wrong? How can you fix it?'"

Jorgen Vig Knudstorp at LEGO said, "In Danish we have an expression that literally translates as, 'managing at eye level,' but it means being able to talk to people on the factory floor, to engineers, to marketers–being at home with everyone."

> **"THE BEST IDEAS COME FROM PEOPLE WHO GET OUT FROM BEHIND THEIR DESKS AND CHAT DIRECTLY WITH OTHERS, LEARN FROM THEM AND BUILD TRUST."**—*Sir Richard Charles Nicholas Branson*

Sir Richard Charles Nicholas Branson, the English business magnate, investor, and philanthropist, is founder of the Virgin Group, which controls more than 400 companies.

These outside advisors only have a limited time to study the situation. It's only by speaking with people who have lived with the problems and have seen it through countless cycles can an understanding be gained. Often these people being interviewed have solutions to the company's problems but are either too frightened to tell the emperor he has no clothes or who, after countless attempts, have given up trying to offer solutions.

As globalization expands and corporate survival becomes even more difficult, only the CEO's with open minds will survive.

ABOUT THE AUTHOR

Jerry Feingold is a highly-sought-after management consultant helping his clients become "globally competitive."

He began independent consulting after retiring from an industry where he worked for 34 years in senior executive positions at four Fortune 100 companies.

Originally an Industrial Engineer, he rose to the executive level where he conducted numerous domestic and international startups and turnarounds.

In addition to speaking engagements at universities and international conferences, Jerry has been featured on Public Televisions and talk radio.

Corporate Homicide? is his third book. His previous books were *Getting Lean* and *Lean Administration*.

He lives in Ventura, California with his wife Ruthann and his Australian Labradoodle, Maddy.

Contact Jerry at www.JerryFeingold.com.

BIBLIOGRAPHY

Feingold, Jerry. *Getting Lean*. WCM Associates, 2005

Feingold, Jerry. *Lean Administration*. WCM Associates, 2008

Halbersham, David, *The Reckoning*. William Morrow and Company, 1986

Imai, Masaaki, *Genba kaizen: a commonsense low-cost approach to management*. New York: McGraw-Hill Professional, 1997

Imai, Masaaki. *Kaizen*. McGraw-Hill, 1986

Maccoby, Michael. *Narcissistic Leaders*, Random House. 2003

Womack, James P. and Jones, Daniel T. *Lean Thinking*. Simon and Schuster, 1996

Womack, James P. and Jones, Daniel T, Roos, Daniel. *The Machine that Changed the World*. 1991

PHOTO CREDITS

Yogi Berra

See page for author [Public domain], <a href="https://commons.wikimedia.org/wiki/File%3AYogi_Berra_1956.png">via Wikimedia Commons</a>

Datsun 14 Roadster

By Morio (Own work) [<a href="http://creativecommons.org/licenses/by-sa/3.0">CC BY-SA 3.0</a>], <a href="https://commons.wikimedia.org/wiki/File%3ADatsun_14_Roadster_front-left_2013_Tokyo_Motor_Show.jpg">via Wikimedia Commons</a>

1934 Ford Roadster

By Pseudopanax at English Wikipedia (Own work) [Public domain], <a href="https://commons.wikimedia.org/wiki/File%3A1934_Ford_Roadster_(Warbirds_%26_Wheels_museum).jpg">via Wikimedia Commons</a>

Datsun Fair lady

By Morio (Own work) [<a href="http://creativecommons.org/licenses/by-sa/3.0">CC BY-SA 3.0</a>], <a href="https://commons.wikimedia.org/wiki/File%3ADatsun_14_Roadster_front-left_2013_Tokyo_Motor_Show.jpg">via Wikimedia Commons</a>

Ghosen

By World Economic Forum from Cologny, Switzerland [CC BY-SA 2.0 (http://creativecommons.org/licenses/by-sa/2.0)], via Wikimedia Commons

Tower Records

By No machine-readable author provided. Mike Dillon assumed (based on copyright claims). [<a href="http://www.gnu.org/copyleft/fdl.html">GFDL</a>, <a href="http://creativecommons.org/licenses/by-sa/3.0/">CC-BY-SA-3.0</a> or <a href="http://creativecommons.org/licenses/by-sa/2.5-2.0-1.0">CC BY-SA 2.5-2.0-1.0</a>], <a href="https://commons.wikimedia.org/wiki/File%3ATower_Records_Sunset.jpg">via Wikimedia Commons</a>

Goose that laid golden egg

iStock-180818520

Legos

By Klasbricks at English Wikipedia (Transferred from en.wikipedia to Commons.) [Public domain], <a href="https://commons.wikimedia.org/wiki/File%3A2_duplo_lego_bricks.jpg">via Wikimedia Commons</a>

One Hour Photo

Istock - 451637349

Kodak Instant Camera

By Malopez 21 (Own work) [<a href="http://creative-commons.org/licenses/by-sa/4.0">CC BY-SA 4.0</a>], <a href="https://commons.wikimedia.org/wiki/File%3AKodak_Instant_Camera%2C_Colorburst_100.jpg">via Wikimedia Commons</a>

New Coke

Istock – 153015899

Google Glass

By Antonio Zugaldia (http://www.flickr.com/photos/azugaldia/7457645618) [<a href="http://creativecommons.org/licenses/by/2.0">CC BY 2.0</a>], <a href="https://commons.wikimedia.org/wiki/File%3AGoogle_Glass_detail.jpg">via Wikimedia Commons</a>

Schwinn Bike

By Photojunkie (Own work) [Public domain], <a href="https://commons.wikimedia.org/wiki/File%3ACarnegie_Science_Center_1950s_Black_Phantom.JPG">via Wikimedia Commons</a>

Monroe Working Woman

By SMU Central University Libraries [<a href="https://www.flickr.com/commons/usage/">No restrictions</a>], <a href="https://commons.wikimedia.org/wiki/File%3A(Woman_working%2C_Monroe_Calculating_Machine_Company)_(6863297446).jpg">via Wikimedia Commons</a>

Monroe calculator

By Monroe (costruttore), Baldwin Frank Stephen (inventore) [<a href="http://creativecommons.org/licenses/by-sa/4.0">CC BY-SA 4.0</a>], <a href="https://commons.wikimedia.org/wiki/File%3A-Calcolatrice_meccanica_-_Museo_scienza_tecnologia_Milano_08804.jpg">via Wikimedia Commons</a>

Computer Mouse

Istock 517939748

Porsche

By Lothar Spurzem Die Bilder bitte nicht ohne Einwilligung des Autors verändern. (Own work) [<a href="http://creativecommons.org/licenses/by-sa/2.0/de/deed.en">CC BY-SA 2.0 de</a>], <a href="https://commons.wikimedia.org/wiki/File%3APorsche_356_A_Speedster_1600_Super%2C_Bj._1956%2C_Heck_(2016-07-02_Sp).jpg">via Wikimedia Commons</a>

Jester

Istock – 176058112

Fisker

2012 Fisker Karma -2012 NYIAS, By IFCAR (Own work) [Public domain], via Wikimedia Commons

Toyotapet Crown -1957 Toyopet crown

By Mytho88 (Own work) [GFDL (http://www.gnu.org/copyleft/fdl.html) or CC BY-SA 3.0 (http://creativecommons.org/licenses/by-sa/3.0)], via Wikimedia Commons

Umbrellas

Istock – 152158299

Konosuke

See page for author [Public domain], <a href="https://commons.wikimedia.org/wiki/File%3AKonosuke_Matsushita_01.jpg">via Wikimedia Commons</a>

ENDNOTES

1   Imai, *Genba kaizen: a commonsense low-cost approach to management.* New York: McGraw-Hill Professional. p. 13. ISBN 978-0-07-031446-7 Masaaki (1997).

2   Yogi Berra, *You Can Observe A Lot By Watching: What I've Learned About Teamwork From the Yankees and Life*, Turner Publishing Company, (2008).

3   Louis V. Gerstner, Jr., *Who Says Elephants Can't Dance? Inside IBM's Historic Turn- around (2002)*, p. 43.

4   Edward Tufte, *The Cognitive Style of PowerPoint: Pitching Out Corrupts Within*, Graphics Press, 2006, p. 56.

5   *Ibid.*

6   Richard Feynman, *Surely, You're Joking Mr. Feynman*, W.W. Norton and Company, p. 127, 1985.

7   Bill Snyder, "Carlos Ghosn: *Five Percent of the Challenge is Strategy, Ninety Percent is Execution*", Insights - Stanford Graduate school of Business, July 9, 2014.

8   *Ibid.*

9   David Hinckley, *Fred Foy, announcer best known for 'The Lone Ranger' intro, dies of natural causes at age 89,* The New York Daily News, December 23, 2010.

10   Saul McLeod, Stanford Prison Experiment, *Simply Psychology* 2017.

11   Kahneman, D. & Tversky, A *"Choices, Values, and Frames". American Psychologist. 39 (4): 341–350. doi:10.1037/0003-066x.39.4.341., (1984).*

12   Scott Campbell and Lauren Davidson, The Telegraph, *Lego Trumps Mattel to become World's top toy maker,* September 4, 2014.

13   *Ibid.*

14   Sherod Robinson, Music Executive turned author: *Ron Fierstein Captures Portrait of The Original Steve Jobs,* Music Row April 9, 2015.

15   Times Staff and Wire Reports, *Polaroid Wins $909 Million From Kodak : Photography: The firms have been involved in a patent-infringement suit for years. Analysts had expected the award to be much larger.* LA Times, October 13, 1990.

16   Samuel Jaberg & Duc-Quang Nguyen, *Six things you should know about the watchmaking industry,* BASEL-WORLD, 2017.

17   Malcolm Gladwell, *Creation Myth, Xerox PARC, Apple, and the truth about innovation,* The New Yorker, May 16, 2011.

18   James P. Womack, Daniel T. Jones, and Daniel Roos, *The Machine That Changed the World,* p 45, Free Press, 1990.

19   Ray Williams, *Why Every CEO Needs a Coach, Executive coaches perform key function for CEOs.,* Psychology Today, Aug 13, 2012.